"Readers of Emilie Griffin's previous meditations on life changes and aging . . . will welcome her ever-deepening explorations in *Green Leaves for Later Years*. Whether reflecting on her own life or relating stories from the lives of figures as diverse as Nelson Mandela, Ruth Bell Graham, Auguste Renoir and others, she challenges us to see aging as a discipline of attention offering a richness of experience and joy generally unimagined in our youth-obsessed culture. Emilie Griffin has become a wise woman; her books are twenty-first-century wisdom literature."

John Leax, professor of English and poet-in-residence, Houghton College

"This book is an honest, hopeful word of encouragement. Emilie Griffin makes it abundantly clear that our later years can be a time of creative adventure. We can discover that friends and gratitude, courage and trust, are truly gifts of God's grace moving us beyond our loss and failure, anxiety and illness. This has been Emilie Griffin's personal experience. She has transcended the constant, crippling pain of rheumatoid arthritis by letting go, being flooded with gratitude, trusting our heavenly Father anew. Consequently, with a host of others, I have been personally nourished by her. Take and read."

Roger Fredrikson, pastor emeritus of First Baptist Church
of Sioux Falls, South Dakota

"Part poet, part spiritual director and at least a small part sly humorist, Emilie Griffin is the perfect person to write about how we can draw from Christian faith and wisdom through the journey of life, especially during the later years. The pages turn easily and her wisdom spills out."

Gary W. Moon, M.Div., Ph.D., executive director,
Dallas Willard Center, Westmont College

"Emilie Griffin writes grittily, wittily and transparently. Her green leaves are Edenic, not the result of naiveté but of continued growth despite physical impediments. For Emilie, pain and transcendence live in the same body. Her challenge, like that of others who have lived a long time, comes from not knowing exactly what lies ahead—life as a kind of open-ended novel, the character still in development, the plot not yet tied off neatly—yet a life for which God has an on-going purpose. Emilie lives out that challenge, that purpose, in this story of amazing grace and faithfulness."

Luci Shaw, author of *Breath for the Bones* and writer-in-residence, Regent College

GREEN *for* LEAVES

LATER YEARS

THE SPIRITUAL PATH

OF WISDOM

EMILIE GRIFFIN

IVP Books

An imprint of InterVarsity Press
Downers Grove, Illinois

InterVarsity Press
P.O. Box 1400, Downers Grove, IL 60515-1426
World Wide Web: www.ivpress.com
E-mail: email@ivpress.com

InterVarsity Press® is the book-publishing division of InterVarsity Christian Fellowship/USA®, a movement of students and faculty active on campus at hundreds of universities, colleges and schools of nursing in the United States of America, and a member movement of the International Fellowship of Evangelical Students. For information about local and regional activities, write Public Relations Dept., InterVarsity Christian Fellowship/USA, 6400 Schroeder Rd., P.O. Box 7895, Madison, WI 53707-7895, or visit the IVCF website at <www.intervarsity.org>.

Unless otherwise noted, Scripture quotations are taken from THE JERUSALEM BIBLE, *copyright ©1966 by Darton, Longman & Todd, Ltd. and Doubleday, a division of Bantam Doubleday Dell Publishing Group, Inc. Reprinted by permission.*

While all stories in this book are true, some names and identifying information in this book have been changed to protect the privacy of the individuals involved.

The excerpt from "September Song" by Edward Petherbridge is used by permission.

Cover design: Cindy Kiple
Interior design: Beth Hagenberg
Images: green skeleton of leaf: ©Olga Demchishina/iStockphoto
   torn paper: ©Gary Alvis/iStockphoto

ISBN 978-0-8308-3565-2

Printed in the United States of America ∞

Library of Congress Cataloging-in-Publication Data has been requested.

P	18	17	16	15	14	13	12	11	10	9	8	7	6	5	4	3	2	1
Y	27	26	25	24	23	22	21	20	19	18	17	16	15	14	13	12		

Contents

PREFACE

*I*t is early in the morning, and I am grateful. Grateful that in this year of grace I took a little of my own medicine and returned with a kind of humility. Well, a kind of humbling, at least—a low-to-the-ground way of remembering what it is to begin again. And again. And again. This is the year I admitted, for example, that I cannot ever find my Bible in the early morning, because the house is filled with Bibles, and not one of them is ever the one I'm after when it is still dark and I want to watch the light come up over the trees. For me the light is Christ.

So I begin again, looking for today's Bible reading electronically this time, pulling the day's Scripture up from the website I have bookmarked as *"hodie,"* which is Latin for "today." It is also the first word of the chant monks use to open the Christmas Day antiphon at second vespers. *Hodie Christus natus est.* Today Christ is born.

This is the first line of Benjamin Britten's "Hodie" in the *Ceremony of Carols*, that beautiful work of almost-chant that long ago swept me into the Christian life. And so each morning now this simple Latin word—*hodie*, "today," "this day"—is my entrance into the beauty of the moment and the life of the Lord. Fittingly, it is in the later years that I claim this phrase as part of the day's opening reading and opening prayer. Why fittingly? Because I am fully present in the moment, in the instant, yet by grace connected fully to the Lord. His word, my action. His touch, my word and world enough. Stretching across the globe itself by grace. My self extended. This word, this time, this instant of prayer, my entry point into the day.

Then, through my window—dawn. I am surrounded by green leaves. Emerging from the ground as ferns, wildly successful plants that tap against my windowpanes when the wind blows. Poking up everywhere, rising again like sap one forgets till spring and all comes once again alive, with Christ, with meaning, my Word, God, Lord of hope and all.

> First light, first prayer
> Now into winking blue I dive for the first sacred word
>   and prayer of the day:
> well it's not blue screen
> (that's a tech term, electronics, all that)
> but it's my screen
> blue
> deep
> winking in pre-dawn light
> which is
> on the whole
> the best time of my day with God.
> (though it could be any time.
> you know how that goes.)
> My bell
> My diving Dell

opens a path
early early
not sure when
sometime before dawn.
blue screen
for me
unlimited future
and just to make it extra nice,
the metaphor,
blue is Our Lady's color,
larkspur,
loveliness,
joy.
Hard to explain.
you had to be there.
But I was there,
it was me
and Jesus
me and Jesus
and the whole world besides.
Heart of Christ
Extending pole to pole
and still farther
into the limitless future
of God's love.

When the above text was written, it was January and bitter cold. The text for the day was from the book of Acts: "We set sail from Troas, making a straight run for Samothrace" (Acts 16:11 NAB). I love this reading, and I love Paul's journeys as ways into the life of God.

Leave Your Chair

"Bill Griffin has gone," I wrote back in January, "onto the board of the Alexandria Museum of Art. I am glad of it. That's my one glimmer of hope in a desolate winter, shaken by illness, a chaotic family Christmas, periods of temporary deafness, surging blood pressure, new medications, unpredictability. Only one answer, I conclude. Get up, leave your chair, stop letting rheumatoid arthritis and its courtesies dominate you. Learn to deflect, charmingly, the constant hum of well-intentioned advice that tells you you are sick and getting sicker and put on the Keds, the ones Wendy says you shouldn't wear because they hurt her feet. Oh yes, you heard me right. I shouldn't wear them because they leave her comfortless."

That's it in a nutshell. Everyone seems to have ideas, thoughts, suggestions about how I should get well. But unless the Keds fit, everyone stumbles. My conclusion is that I have to stretch into my recovery. Without being too demanding or officious, I have to take charge. Until you take charge of your own recovery, until you intend to get well, you won't. Intending to get well isn't the same as getting well, but it's a start.

Here is what Oliver Sacks has to say about adaptation in the later years: "Whether it is by learning a new language, traveling to a new place, developing a passion for beekeeping or simply thinking about an old problem in a new way, all of us can find ways to stimulate our brains to grow, in the coming year and those to follow. Just as physical activity is essential to maintaining a healthy body, challenging one's brain, keeping it active, engaged, flexible and playful, is not only fun. It is essential to cognitive fitness."

Oliver Sacks encourages me. I find that his explorations of the worst-case scenarios, in which people have had scary experiences of brain failure, unexplained brain failure, are not depressing but encouraging. These clever *New Yorker* stories of his may look like entertainment to some. But to me, wrestling with all the uncertainties of the later years, Sacks is optimism itself.

I pause to reflect on what lies ahead. This is a big year for me as I turn seventy-five and try to decide what part of me is ready to rest and what part ready to rise and shine.

I make a list of the things that have happened since last year. Not the best things but the most significant things, things that have marked off the months and days. And I find they are few.

- Bill Vaswig's newsletter, in which he accepts his approaching death.

- Gratitude for knowing Bill Vaswig and working with him.

- Thanksgiving and Christmas (chaotic, confusing).

- Epiphany, and the chance to speak of it at the Renovaré Institute in Menlo Park.

- The Chrysostom Society meeting in the Hill Country of Texas.

- The health scare involving Luci Shaw.

The list trails off. At my age—did I say I am seventy-five this year?—I hear a lot of "athlete talk" about pushing past the pain. I think about my editors and readers who have said, "Tell us more about your pain." I hope in these pages I can respond to that question, maybe even be glad of such questions at last.

Hard. It's hard, admitting to myself that spirituality can

make a difference. My evaluation of the preceding year has begun after a week of teaching the spiritual life. And speaking is sometimes euphoric. When you teach the spiritual life you believe you are living it. What you sometimes don't realize is that you, like all those in your audience, need to live each day as a new beginning. In the spiritual life there are no time-outs, no free passes. Everyone has to begin, and begin again.

So I name it all: The gift of pain. The challenge of illness and other surprises. The relentless march of birthdays, joyful yet wistful because they mark off time. My own inadequacy dealing with seas of paperwork. Losing a cherished letter in the whole post-Christmas rush. Bursts of insight and gratitude—for *Conversations*, a wonderful Christian journal, for friends near and far (the season brings them to mind—James Catford, friend in Christ; Kate Campbell, grace maker; Jan Peterson, friend, encourager). The bah-humbug side of Christmas. Recovery, my own, because I have to begin again. Admitting to myself that Christmas is not always peaceful, that family connections are sometimes chaotic. The sorrow of it, taking the fall—that is, accepting my own inadequacy and my need to begin again.

Some weeks later, after days of new beginnings, another list emerges. This time it's more of a gratitude list, but not without dark spots. "Amazing Bill Griffin," the list begins. Then next I write the title of his novel, *Dill of the Nile*. March 25th, Feast of the Annunciation, is the publishing date for *Dill*. I begin to understand that part of me is unhinged by the flood of feelings released by the holidays—concerns about people in far-off places, friends I can't always visit in person but don't want to lose. Then there are friends and colleagues facing death—like our friend Father Val, a Dominican priest in his eighties, brilliantly transcending his illness though it is a constant fact of life for him.

A Spirituality for the Later Years

Some years ago one of the best modern writers on the life cycle, Erik Erikson (1902–1994), realized that he was starting to outlive his categories. He had identified seven stages of life, had written and studied and taught about them extensively, but the longevity of modern people was beginning to outstrip his analysis.

So he began to write and speak about the years after age sixty-five as new and adventurous territory. He applied many of the life lessons he had already discovered and came up with some new ones. The word "wisdom" continually appeared in his writing. But also he wanted to correct the stereotypes of old age and offer a freedom to reinterpret these later stages of living.

My central theme in this book is how Christian faith informs us in the life journey, especially in later years. From time to time I will also touch on my own struggle with illness, a wide array of autoimmune diseases. I don't want to dwell on the pain. But the pain is real. I don't want to suppose that if I just don't think about it, it will go away. I want to show where my encouragement comes from: how God speaks in my life. Especially I am encouraged by Jeremiah 17, which tells us that the righteous person is like a tree planted by living water, whose leaves stay green.

In writing this book I have learned a good deal through observation, reading and study, conversing with others and simply through my own experience and reflection. The words I like best to deal with this stage of life are "transcendence" and "adaptation." My focus is on a person's quest to live deeply and well. My delight has been to raise good questions. Does later life have meaning? Should people continue to work? Should their work change or shift in some way? How important is the creative side of living? What about lifelong learning? What is a good fundamental attitude about change and diminishment? Should society change to accommodate these new "elders"?

The Hidden Spot

Sometimes I think there is a hidden spot in the universe where God is to be found, God and the whole rest of the world besides. It is a sort of Aladdin's cave of memory, joy and courage where all the spiritual gifts glitter in the darkness and every jewel shines.

When I first set out to offer God the best I had, I reflected on an image: the apples of my experience ripening, falling, scattering on the ground. I pictured myself entering into my future with all the hopes and gratitude of a life well lived, trying to gather all the golden apples of the Spirit, the beauties God had bestowed on me.

The years ahead would be my new territory—years of joy and sorrow and uncertainty in the uncharted country of the heart with the Lord himself as my guide. Day by day I would follow this shadowy figure on the path. Sometimes Jesus would walk beside me; sometimes he would climb the rock just ahead and wait for me to catch up, battling with forces of fear and death like Gandalf at the crag of doom. Sometimes I would imagine Jesus as a twelve-year-old, a youth barely older than a child but already wise and able to explain to his elders the meaning of God's plan.

That was my Jesus, and I would follow him.

I sat in a coffeehouse and attempted to capture—like a sketch artist who works quickly because the light is fading and the sun will soon be down—the vision I had seen, the glimpse into the meaning of existence that is the writer's only spiritual treasure.

Then fear closed in. Fear and self-doubt, my ancient enemies: *Who do you think you are, to bring the golden apples of God's wisdom to the world? To the bystanders, the wayfarers, the random readers who riffle the pages and put the book down? Who declared you the keeper of the universe?*

Then I knew for sure that the Lord was with me. At every step of the long journey that is the later years, he has accompanied me. There are many who tell me they do not know the Lord, that he has never walked with them, never offered a wafer of comfort along the hard and perilous way. And I tell them, "Wait."

Wait until all earthly consolations and comforts fall away. Wait until the constellations that once populated the night sky fade and the universe seems to grow cold. Think, always, that when you are exhausted and drained from the long trudge of existence, there will be golden apples on the ground, scattered randomly but wonderfully ripe. Never hesitate to think, *The Lord put this one here just for me.* It is an old story, and the Lord never seems to stop telling it. It is a story of encouragement, confidence and love.

I am conscious of the passing of years. As I move into the future I am conscious of all the coffeehouse reflections of the past—discarded pages, lists and notes that have long ago vanished into the muddle of whatever I did to serve him, whatever I did to confront my own monsters on the crag, whatever I did to harvest the apples and scatter them to the world, to the random wayfarers with whom I stopped to share a bite.

What wisdom do I bring to the later years?

Nothing more than the wisdom of dwelling in the present moment. No more than the courage of God's promises. Nothing more than the perseverance to walk through sorrow. No more than the unlimited future of God's love.

Emilie Griffin
Feast of Saint Michael and All Angels
Alexandria, Louisiana

1

Pushing Past the Pain

The fear of the LORD is the beginning of wisdom,
and the knowledge of the Holy One is insight.
For by me your days will be multiplied,
and years will be added to your life.

Proverbs 9:10-11 ESV

I grow old . . . I grow old . . .
I shall wear the bottoms of my trousers rolled.

T. S. Eliot

*Y*ou could live to be ninety," my doctor said.

"Really?" I answered. He had gotten my attention.

We were discussing the distortion of my hands from rheumatoid arthritis. The doctor wanted me to consider surgery on my hands. At least he wanted me to investigate it. But for me, the revelation was that he thought I might live to my ninetieth birthday. Up to that point I had never considered such a long life.

Even though I am older than I ever planned to be, I don't spend a lot of time thinking about old age. In fact, I avoid the idea of "old age," which for me connotes weakness, decline, debility, loss of faculties and maybe a certain distortion of vision. I have, in short, accepted without realizing it (without intending it) most of the caricatures of old age. Rather dark humor accompanies this phase of life. "What's the alternative?" people say jokingly, but the joking has an edge.

There's another way of looking at the later years: not as old age but long life. Scripture speaks of these later years as a gift from God, a reward from him. Our lives are extended by God because we are wise, having gained in knowledge and insight. But what does this mean on a practical level about how we are to live? What do we do with the gift, the blessing, the quandary and challenge of long life?

I went to see the hand doctor about a possible surgery. He took x-rays. He studied my case. He talked to me about how I use my hands, what kinds of things I can still do. He told me what surgery might accomplish; he also explained what couldn't be corrected and what damage would remain. I kept repeating that my doctor had suggested the surgery.

"But do you want the surgery?" the hand doctor asked.

"I'm not sure."

"We should do the surgery not when he wants it but when you want it," he said. In the meantime, we agreed, he would monitor my situation. That visit was at least three years ago, and as far as I can tell my hands are the same.

True, there are certain negatives about growing older. Physical decline is a big issue. Still, I think the larger challenge of old age is not physical but spiritual. How are we to transcend the obstacles of the later years? How should we imagine long life? How can we cherish and value the gift of long life? What kind of people does God mean for us to be? What do we desire and intend for ourselves during the later years of our lives?

During my reflections I decided to look for examples of long life well-lived. And I resolved to consult the Bible for its wisdom on the later years.

A Long Life

On February 11, 2010, a great celebration was held in South Africa and around the world in honor of Nelson Mandela, then ninety-two. Great crowds remembered the moment twenty years earlier when Mandela was released from prison. He was hailed as the heroic figure who brought down the rule of apartheid. British prime minister Gordon Brown remembered that moment as a defining event of our times.

Thousands remembered Mandela walking to freedom after twenty-seven years of incarceration. They recalled him stepping out of the Cape Town prison, then called Victor Verster, holding hands with his wife Winnie, a figure of defiance in her own right. A ten-foot-high bronze statue erected on the site in 2008 depicts Mandela's return to freedom: his fist raised, but smiling and determined to enjoy this amazing moment.

"We knew that his freedom meant our freedom had also arrived," Cyril Ramaphosa told the assembled crowds at the prison twenty years later. Ramaphosa had been a leader in Mandela's African National Congress (ANC) and headed a committee that welcomed Mandela back to freedom in 1990. On this day of commemoration he and other ANC leaders reenacted Mandela's historic walk from the gates of the prison, linking arms and shouting, "Viva Mandela!" But Winnie Madikizela-Mandela decided not to join the reenactment. It would have been too painful, she explained. She and Nelson Mandela were divorced in 1996.

Four years after his release from prison, Mandela was elected South Africa's first black president. He served just one five-year term, hoping to establish a precedent of democratically elected leadership that would be a contrast to the dictatorships and power-mongering elsewhere in Africa and the world. In his life as well as in his rhetoric, Mandela denounced fraud and violence. He also championed racial reconciliation, encouraging a peaceful transition of power for his beloved country. Mandela is a professing Christian, not only raised by Wesleyans in Africa but embracing his Christian faith over a lifetime. He has stated that his Christian faith helped him to endure his long imprisonment.

Since Mandela's election in 1994, his ANC party has made great strides in reducing poverty. Houses have been built. Water, electricity and schools have been provided for blacks who never had them under apartheid. But great gaps remain between the rich and the poor. And now there is another irony. Some blacks are rich, including new black entrepreneurs, while others are poor.

Even so, Nelson Mandela can see how in his one lifespan he made a beginning. He knows what he did with his energy, commitment and time. For him, the gift of long life has allowed him to see and take consolation in South Africa's achievements during his lifetime.

Mandela was born from an African royal strain, though he was not eligible for kingship. His lifelong struggle for justice and better living conditions for his people makes one wonder whether the ancient notion of kingship has merit after all. Like Henry V in Shakespeare's play, Mandela went among his people in disguise as it were, asking few privileges for himself, working in menial jobs and struggling to be educated as a lawyer and gain accreditation. After becoming a lawyer he worked on behalf of blacks who could not afford costly legal representation. His whole concern seems to have been for justice. Throughout much of his early career he was an armed activist fighting against apartheid. Charged with sabotage, he was tried and convicted in the South African courts and sent to jail. During his long imprisonment he worked at hard labor and received poor rations but nevertheless studied law via correspondence and gained prominence as a political figure even in jail. This is a man who transcended difficulties and overcame obstacles.

Mandela has received 250 awards and honors, including the 1993 Nobel Peace Prize. In 2009 the United Nations General Assembly voted to establish his birthday, July 18, as Mandela Day, honoring his contribution to world freedom.

Morgan Freeman, the American actor, played Mandela in the film *Invictus*. It was a role he long aspired to, he told *The Guardian*; his challenge was not only to offer a realistic portrayal of a man still living, but also to humanize Mandela since he was already of such heroic and mythical stature. Freeman worked to show Mandela's limitations yet also convey the inspirational quality of his leadership.

Such humanizing is a worthwhile effort. After all, the patriarchs were human. Abraham and Sarah were human. They had weaknesses and gave way to them. But their lives had tremendous impact and force. Their weaknesses made their strengths more believable. They inspired—and continue to inspire—many generations after them.

An Extra Decade

When someone lives to be ninety-two, we're inclined to think he has been granted an extra decade. In fact, that's what the Bible says: "For by me your days will be multiplied, and years will be added to your life" (Prov 9:11 ESV). However, what matters isn't so much the accomplishments of those ten years. What counts the most is the perspective gained, both for those who live long and others who observe them. Time extended lets us see the arc of a life, what the trajectory of that life is reaching for, where it seems to be heading and, maybe, what that life has meant.

When I picture these extra years of long life I don't immediately think of a happy, fulfilled person sitting in a rocking chair and receiving visitors. Instead, what comes to mind is more like a chase scene in a movie with Matt Damon playing Jason Bourne. The driver is maneuvering against oncoming traffic, and the likelihood of collision is high. With split-second timing he swerves to avoid obstacles, but his instincts are amazingly sure. The accumulated experience of a lifetime gives him very sharp judgment, uncanny skill. He moves with a kind of dead-on certainty toward what he is chasing. Life, in this scenario, is an obstacle course, and the winners are those who skirt the worst of it.

At the same time the person in question gives way to reality. He or she can't predict exactly what lies ahead. The oncoming traffic of existence is part of the joy, part of the challenge and excitement. Not only that: the heart surrenders and lets go.

Two older people I have worked with in Renovaré are William Vaswig and Roger Fredrikson. Vaswig, a Lutheran pastor and prayer-healer, died in his late seventies after dealing for many years with a heart ailment. Fredrikson, a pastor who recently turned ninety, has struggled with various forms of cancer. Sometimes he is in remission. Some-times the cancer returns. Always Fredrickson lives joyfully with simple trust in God.

Both of these men are known for strong faith. Their con-stant drive along the obstacle course of living seems to show unerring skill. I have loved being with them to share their childlike vitality and joy. Both men have reminded me to enjoy the adventure of living, to relish the unexpected. I think it is all about trust—how they have trusted God with the arc of their lives, the trajectory of their existence.

Not to mention loving the Bible. I enjoyed their keen love of the Bible and personal style of prayer, like they were having a constant conversation with God. They joked and laughed, sometimes even danced. They liked to clown around, especially with a friendly audience around them. Since Bill's death, I am glad to say, the whole Renovaré circle has continued this delightful personal style of prayer.

Lately, in some of the conversations surrounding justice for women in our time, the word "patriarchal" has lost its luster. But William Vaswig and Roger Fredrikson struck me as being patriarchs in the best possible way. Patriarchs go before us and clear a path for our dreams and aspira-tions. They have long life and we call it a blessing from God. Jesus speaks about this kind of patriarchy in a long passage in the Gospel of John. In John 8:31-59 he promises that the truth will set his listeners free. Some are puzzled by this claim. "We are descendants of Abraham, and have never been slaves to anyone," they respond. In other words, "Why do we need to be set free?" Jesus must explain to them what spiritual freedom really is. But there's another undercurrent here. These Jews are also challenging Jesus' authority and his ability to make promises such as these.

Finally Jesus says, "Your ancestor Abraham rejoiced that he would see my day; he saw it and was glad." The bystanders challenge him: "You are not yet fifty years old, and have you seen Abraham?" Jesus answers them, saying, "Very truly, I tell you, before Abraham was, I am."

This text is generally taken to mean that Jesus was revealing his divinity, his descent from Abraham and his existence before the time of Abraham. Of course, the term "I Am" is one of the Hebrew names for the godhead. No need to stop and elaborate further. It's enough to remember that Abraham is the ancestor of Judaism, Christianity and Islam and that Christians acknowledge Jesus as God. In our reflections on God's will for us we will continue to make reference to both Jesus and Abraham.

Abraham and Sarah: Learning Trust
Searching through my inventory of mentors, I could find no one better to personify long life than Abraham and Sarah. They have given us the example of what it is to live long and well. Abraham and Sarah are my teachers of long life. Reflecting on their life stories I hope to tease out motifs and scenarios that will help us ponder the meaning of long life.

Abraham's name is first given as "Abram," which means either "exalted father" or "my father is exalted." Later his name is changed to "Abraham." This business of changing names is a way of signifying a passage of faith. Abram's wife is named "Sarai" but her name is changed to "Sarah," also indicating a passage of faith.

The name "Abraham" also makes reference to Abraham's destiny: He is to become the father of many nations. Apparently there's no real root for this in the Hebrew, but the biblical text assigns this meaning to Abraham's change of name.

There's still a third speculation on what "Abraham" may mean: "The father loves." This connotes the love of God our Father. It also signifies Abraham's own loving nature as a father and his consent to become the father of many nations.

Abram's story begins in his home country, Ur of the Chaldees (Gen 11:28), a Sumerian city in the Euphrates Valley near the head of the Persian Gulf. Abram's father Terah leaves Ur along with Abram and his wife Sarai (later "Sarah"), who go up the river with their flocks and herds until they come to Haran, a trading center in northern Aram (now Syria). The family settles there, and later on Abram's father Terah dies. This departure from his home country is the beginning of Abraham's journey of faith.

I admire Abram's faith in trusting God with his life. Then it occurs to me that everyone is called to do what Abram did, to trust God with his or her life. How do we put our trust in God? Realistically, what does that mean?

Reflections, Questions and a Prayer

Many of us dread the prospect of old age rather than looking forward to it as something to enjoy. But the Bible speaks of long life as a reward from God. How does this idea hold good for us today?

This chapter examines the meaning of long life, along with ways that we might aspire to live well. The author tells us of her own surprise at the possibility of living long. Have you experienced surprise at the idea of living into old age? How do you feel about the expression "old age"?

This chapter mentions individuals in modern life who are

much admired and have lived long lives. Nelson Mandela, for example, conceived a life dream in youth and continued to pursue it in the later years. Do you have such a life dream? Has your dream changed over time? How is your faith intertwined with this dream?

Abraham and Sarah are discussed as good biblical examples of what it is to live long. According to the Bible, their lives were very long and they had to take risks in leaving their homeland at God's command. How does their story shape your understanding of the risk of living, and living long?

Even though Jesus' earthly life ended at age thirty-three, Christians believe that Jesus is alive and can be present to us. Have you considered Jesus as a teacher of long life?

Prayer

Lord, please give me a sense of the vital meaning of long life. Help me to see it as your reward. Help me to avoid thoughts and phrases that describe long life as burdensome or unimportant. Give me the insight to honor those who have lived long and to treasure my later years.

2

Blue Skies, Gray Skies

Questions Without Answers

Happy are those who find wisdom,
and those who get understanding,
for her income is better than silver,
and her revenue better than gold.
She is more precious than jewels,
and nothing you desire can compare with her.
Long life is in her right hand;
in her left hand are riches and honor.

Proverbs 3:13-16 NRSV

And all shall be well and
All manner of thing shall be well

Julian of Norwich

*T*his past year has been a little tougher than most of them," Bill Vaswig wrote in his newsletter for July 2010. I had been shuffling through the mail, but when I opened this message I settled back in the chair near the front door.

"I have been in the hospital numerous times and have received a total of fourteen units of blood over the past twelve months. I've had sixteen pounds of water removed from my body and received three more stents (added to the sixteen I already had). Presently I'm on thirteen medications daily to manage my health."

Usually I'm not eager to hear recitations like this one, about stents and medications and blood transfusions. But when it's Bill Vaswig, I pay attention.

Bill was one of the most upbeat and cheerful people I have known. He was founder and president of Preaching and Prayer Ministries, an organization dedicated to emotional and physical healing. An ordained Lutheran minister (Evangelical Lutheran Church of America) and author, Bill lived in Issaquah, Washington. He was trained in Christian healing by Agnes Sanford, whose methods deeply impressed him and many others. Though he had long been a Christian pastor, this healing ministry was new territory for him. I heard him in one of his healing workshops, and I realized not only how effective they were, but how simple and humble Bill was about Christian healing prayer.

I first met Bill in 1994 when I joined the Renovaré ministry team. For several years I did not know about his work as a Christian healer, how he went far and wide on this platform with the likes of Matthew and Dennis Linn and Francis McNutt and how he was involved in charismatic renewal. I just knew him as a simple, good, prayerful person. Later I knew him as a man who bore his sufferings and health issues with real Christian patience and joy.

When he was in his late seventies, Bill wrote a newsletter that he sent out to a few fortunate folks. I was one of them. In it he talked about his own struggles, such as the fourteen units of blood received, three stents added to the sixteen he already had and thirteen medications daily to manage his health. How did that make him feel?

"In spite of the hospitalizations and treatment," he wrote, "I am feeling excellent at this present moment. The Lord is good. He enables me to keep working but has kindly signaled me to 'slow down.'"

That's my idea of gratitude. In spite of his health issues Bill Vaswig said, "The Lord is good." What was his idea of slowing down? Well, he explains it.

"From now on I will be thrilled to do three missions a year. If you want me to come I am able, God willing. I have had 272 missions (usually lasting three days) at churches, colleges, seminaries and camps in the past thirty-four years. I will also reduce the number of people I see in my office for prayer to three a week. People come from all parts of the country for prayer, and I am happy to pray for them."

What accounted for Bill Vaswig's cheerfulness? Surely his close friendship with Jesus Christ. He expressed this joy in dozens of ways.

"I am becoming more peaceful and more aware of Christ's presence. His 'Lo, I am with you always', even to the end of the world' is more real. I am learning to 'wait on the Lord' by sitting in silence. All of my own illness has brought me closer to God."

In his newsletter Vaswig spoke of silent prayer as a source of comfort and strength, quoting David Benner on the stillness created by silent prayer and the importance of centering ourselves in God. This for him was the place of divine transformation.

Abraham and Sarah as Role Models

What is it about prayer? How does it strengthen people, make them willing to take a chance? Two of my favorite Bible people, Abraham and Sarah, were people of prayer, although the Bible doesn't describe their journey so much in terms of prayer as of confidence in God. Take the story of how they left their homeland and set out on a journey in faith.

Abram and Sarai had already left Ur of the Chaldees and moved to Haran, a trading center in northern Syria. The family settled there, along with Abram's herds, flocks and entourage. But the Lord didn't let them pause for long. After Abram's father, Terah, died, the Lord spoke to Abram and asked him to move once more: "Go from your country and your kindred and your father's house to the land that I will show you" (Gen 12:1 NRSV).

Obviously Abram had a close relationship with the Lord. The Bible does not mention any glory shining round, no burning bush, but it's clear that Abram could recognize God's authentic voice speaking to him and converse with him. The closeness of their relationship is plain. But God also made explicit and practical demands. His requirements were clear. Abram was not allowed to settle down fully. He was not able to put down roots and spread out. God had a particular future in mind for him, a destiny. And he sweetened all this with a promise of reward, to make of Abram's descendants "a great nation" (Gen 12:2).

Real trust was needed for Abram to accept this command and this promise. Remember, at that point he had no descendants, and his wife Sarai was barren. Still he trusted God. He obeyed in faith. He pulled up stakes and journeyed for a second time. With Sarai and his nephew Lot he traveled to Canaan, and when he reached Shechem (modern-day Nablus), he built an altar there. Then he built another altar a little farther on, in

Bethel, slightly north of Jerusalem. There the Lord appeared again, and this time he said he would give this land to Abram's descendants (Gen 12:7). That was the command. And that was the promise. The Lord kept appearing and repeating this promise throughout Abram's lifetime. How amazing it must have been to hear such a promise.

Still, Abram and his entourage had to keep traveling because there was a famine in the land. They went on moving southwest, heading toward Egypt where grain was plentiful. People from everywhere fled into Egypt, which they thought of as a granary for emergency supplies. Once in Egypt, further complications arose.

Ruth Bell Graham

When I try to imagine what Abraham's wife Sarah was like, I think of Ruth Bell Graham (1920–2007). She was born in Qingjiang, Kiangsu, China, as Ruth McCue Bell, the child of Presbyterian medical missionaries stationed at the Presbyterian hospital three hundred miles north of Shanghai. Her parents, Dr. and Mrs. L. Nelson Bell, had five children; Ruth was the second. She started high school at age thirteen in Pyongyang, Korea, now North Korea, and studied three years there. She finished high school in Montreat, North Carolina, where her parents were on furlough. At Wheaton College in Wheaton, Illinois, she met Billy Graham, who was amazed by her. He could hardly believe that someone could be so spiritual and so beautiful, too.

What Billy noticed most was that Ruth consulted God about everything. She told him at one point that she dedicated Saturday nights to prayer and study, in preparation for the Lord's day. What kind of college girl would say a thing like that? Ruth Bell would, and young Billy thought he would need to be creative to get a date with her. So they went to hear an afternoon performance of Handel's *Messiah* in Wheaton's Pierce Chapel on a cold and snowy Sunday. Afterward over a cup of tea they had a chance to talk. That evening Ruth went home and prayed, reviewing the entire situation with the Lord Almighty. She had made her mind up. Billy Graham was the man. But she needed God's blessing and providence to make it happen.

Later, when he learned about Ruth's impetuous and fervent prayer, Billy was surprised. If Ruth had made her mind up that night, why did she keep him guessing for so long? Many young men in Wheaton admired her. He wasn't even remotely sure she would say yes just to spending more time with him—after it had taken Billy a month even to ask her for a date.

Courtship and Marriage

Ruth admired Amy Carmichael and was determined that she and Billy would become missionaries to Tibet. Billy wasn't so sure. But they worked things out since it seemed they were made for each other. The pair easily gained their parents' approval and married in 1943. But in Ruth's attempts to turn Billy into a Tibetan missionary, she realized he was stubborn and strong-willed. Other than God, no one would tell him what to do.

After marrying, the couple lived in the Chicago area, then moved to Montreat, North Carolina, where Ruth's parents had settled after they fled China to avoid the Communist takeover of power. She remained in Montreat the rest of her life, eventually making a rustic mountainside home called

Little Piney Cove the family's homestead. As Billy developed into a major evangelist with a worldwide ministry, Ruth stayed home for the most part, caring for their five children. Graham later wrote in his autobiography of his regrets about being an absentee father and the effects on his family. But Ruth, always a traditionalist in her values, accepted her role as homemaker and homebody.

Alone for much of the time while her husband was away, Ruth made efforts to stay intellectually keen. She was an avid reader and writer. In Ruth Graham's biography, Patricia Cornwell wrote that "it was common for her to have 20 or 30 books scattered around the house, each in some stage of being read." Cornwell added, "Finishing a book just because she had started it, she once said, 'was like going into the pantry and thinking you had to eat all the peas before you could open anything else.'" Over her lifetime Ruth wrote fourteen books. Some were poetry, some were memoirs, all were shaped by her deep attachment to the Bible and to her family life.

Mrs. Graham chose the life she led. She conveyed inner peace, as this comment to *Ladies Home Journal* shows: "I knew from the very beginning that I would never be first place in his life," she said. "Christ would be first." Still, she was independent-minded. Even though she was the wife of a famous Baptist minister, she remained a loyal Presbyterian all her life.

Billy and Ruth were married more than sixty years, until Ruth's death at age eighty-nine. Throughout the marriage she was Billy's advisor, counselor, companion and comforter. Though she herself preferred a supportive role, she became a powerful presence to many, especially when she was able to travel with her husband. My husband and I visited briefly with Ruth at the San Antonio Billy Graham Crusade in 1997. While her role was behind the scenes, it was widely known how much her opinion mattered to Billy.

For the last decade of her life Ruth was disabled by severe ailments. She suffered from degenerative osteoarthritis of the back and neck and was bedridden and finally comatose at the Grahams' home in the mountains of western North Carolina. In anticipation of her own death she wrote a poem, part of which was quoted in the *New York Times*:

Then the goodbyes come
again again
like a small death,
the closing of a door.

The day before Ruth's death, Billy Graham released a statement through the Billy Graham Evangelistic Association stating, "Ruth is my soul mate and best friend, and I cannot imagine living a single day without her by my side. I am more and more in love with her today than when we first met over 65 years ago as students at Wheaton College."

The Gift of Remembering

One of the great blessings of long life is the chance to look back and make sense of things. Both Ruth and Billy Graham wrote accounts of their lives and enlisted others to help them with the writing. They knew the power of reflection. They also understood the importance of the example they were setting for others.

But at the same time they were modest people. It's easy to assume that people like the Grahams must have strongly developed egos—which is no doubt true. They needed the stamina and confidence to sustain long years in the public sphere. But both Billy and Ruth Graham were reluctant to be held up as saints. They knew their failings and the dangers of arrogance.

Even from a distance I got a sense of Ruth's quick wit and charm. When my husband, William Griffin, was invited to work as an editor on Billy Graham's autobiography, *Just As I Am*, he was invited to Montreat to meet the Grahams. When the book's subject walked into the room, along with his wife, my husband addressed him as "Dr. Graham."

"Please, call me Billy," he replied. My husband said he couldn't do that.

"Why ever not?" the Grahams wanted to know.

"It would be like calling the pope 'Chuck,'" my husband said, referring to Pope John Paul II, whose real first name was Karol, or Charles. A certain amount of laughter followed.

"Well, that's fine, *Mr.* Griffin," Mrs. Graham replied with a smile, displaying her egalitarian style.

What are we to learn from Ruth Bell Graham? I think we can see parallels between her life and that of Sarah, Abraham's wife. In one sense Ruth Graham was modest and supportive of her husband's work. In another sense she exerted prophetic leadership, moving strongly into the future.

Abraham, Sarah and the Covenant

Abraham is honored as the father of faith by three different religions: Judaism, Christianity and Islam. According to Jewish tradition, he was born about 1800 B.C. One story tells of how Abram challenged his father Terah, an idol merchant, about the foolishness of idol worship. One day when

Terah was out, young Abram took a hammer and smashed all the idols in the home except the largest. Abram then placed the hammer in the hand of the largest idol. When his father came back and asked what Abram had done, the son said, "The idols got into a fight, and the big one smashed all the others."

His father answered, "Don't be ridiculous. These idols have no life or power. They can't do anything."

Abram replied, "Then why do you worship them?"

This story isn't found in the Bible. It's part of midrash, the Jewish storytelling tradition. But it fits perfectly with what is in the Bible: that Abram believed in the one true God. In Genesis 12 we read how the Creator spoke to Abram and made him an offer. If he would leave his birthplace and travel to a far country, God would bless him and make him a great nation. Abram accepted this offer, and the covenant (*berit*) between God and the Jewish people was sealed.

Abraham endured many tests of faith to prove himself worthy of this covenant. Leaving his home was one of these trials. Raised a city-dweller, he had to adopt a nomad's life, traveling through what is now the land of Israel for many years—land that God promised to Abraham's descendants. Sarah is also part of this foundational story. The Abraham stories are also Sarah stories. Sarah supported her husband in many ways, even before she could bear him a child. Many narratives convey this throughout their long life together.

Do we know why Abraham and Sarah lived to such ad-vanced ages? Scholars are divided about the ages specified in the Bible accounts. But we need not concern ourselves with these questions. Let's simply take the Bible accounts at face value. When Abram was one hundred and Sarai ninety, God promised Abram a son by Sarai, changing Abram's name to Abraham (father of many), and Sarai's to Sarah (from "my princess" to "princess"). Sure enough, Sarah eventually bore Abraham a son, Isaac, a name derived from the word "laughter," expressing Abraham's joy at having a son in his old age (Gen 17–18). Abraham lived to one hundred seventy-five. I'd like to think that spiritual life—cultivating friendship with God—is what strengthened Abraham and Sarah to remain steadfast and constant in the later years of change.

How Does Spiritual Life Make A Difference?

What do we mean by the spiritual life anyhow? Today many people bandy the term "spirituality" about, but they clearly mean different things. Christians use the phrase "spiritual formation" to refer to a life of discipline, including such practices as fasting, prayer, study, service, submission, simplicity and solitude. The point of a spiritual life is to be in dialogue with God, in conversation with him, and to see the world under his sovereignty and governed by his love. To know this vividly—as Abraham and Sarah did, as the Grahams did—is to be open to a full, creative life. The life of spiritual formation strengthens us for the challenge of later years. God is with us. Who can be against us?

We find remarkably spiritual people all around us. They are humble. They are modest. Sometimes, like Jesus, they pass into the crowd (see Jn 8:59). Often we can guess at their spiritual practice: prayer, meditation, fasting, study, simplicity, solitude, submission, service and all the rest. They fly below the radar. It's hard to pick them out in a crowd. Even Jesus didn't look so remarkable. The Roman soldiers needed Judas to point him out to them. To some he looked like any other Galilean.

Even so we need to keep such holy people constantly in our sights. These spiritually transformed people will inspire us. They will help us to live effectively and well, even in our later years. Just when we think our lives are over, when we think it's time to sit exhaustedly in a chair, such people encourage us. They are our Abrahams. Our Sarahs. They help us to be evergreen, producing green leaves in our late years.

Turning Ninety, but How?

In her 1999 memoir, *Time to Be in Earnest*, the author P. D. James wrote, "If 77 is a time to be in earnest, eighty is a time to recognize old age, accepting with such fortitude as one can muster its inevitable pains, inconvenience and indignities and rejoicing in its few compensations."

More recently, a *USA Today* reporter interviewed James for her ninetieth birthday, observing, "Today, James still emanates an aura of contentment and a zest for life." When the reporter asked James about that air of contentment, she replied, "I should have, shouldn't I, my dear? I've had a very happy life. There have been bad moments in it. Some very bad moments. But one comes through the bad moments. Every night I say a prayer of gratitude for the day that has passed and for still being here."

Gratitude. Thankfulness puts us in touch with God's grace. That's the sustaining energy of the spiritual life, holding us up and holding us together in the later years. Often we think we must actively work in the world, practicing discipline and making things change for the better. But gratitude—that is, waiting on the grace of God, letting the grace of Christ fall upon us—is the essential value. Ruth Graham shows us this. Billy Graham, especially in his later years, gives us the same example. And they are following in the prophetic footsteps of Abraham and Sarah.

Reflections, Questions and a Prayer

This chapter is about the spiritual life, but the issue of physical illness is important too. We meet Bill Vaswig, a Lutheran pastor and healer who had numerous stents in his heart, and learn about how his relationship to Jesus Christ strengthened him for the challenges of living. Billy and Ruth Graham are also mentioned. Again, we see how a strong faith commitment is vital to the business of long life. Abraham and Sarah are revealed as fine examples of the late-in-life journey. And P. D. James, the British mystery novelist, gives one clue to a strong spiritual life: gratitude.

Make a list of several things in your life that you are grateful for. Can you identify other aspects of the spiritual life that will help to strengthen you for the journey?

Prayer

Lord, teach me to practice the spiritual life as my years demand and dictate. If I am physically hampered, and can't kneel as I used to do, help me to let go of that. Teach me new ways of prayer and discipline that fit with my situation. Help me to grow closer to you and to love others, too.

3

STRETCHING
TOWARD HAPPINESS

I have set before you life and death, blessings and curses.
Choose life so that you and your descendants may live,
loving the LORD your God, obeying him, and holding fast to him;
for that means life to you and length of days.

Deuteronomy 30:19-20 NRSV

*C*an we find our happiness by stretching toward it? Can we laugh our way into greater health and happiness? Many voices say yes.

One of the great sayings in my husband's family was characteristically Irish-American: "It's a great life if you don't weaken." For a long time I heard this saying without knowing that for my in-laws, weakening meant regression into pain.

Whenever anyone said this, everyone else would laugh. The laughter was an acknowledgment of the wisdom of it all. Or as my Irish-American friend John Rogan once explained, "We're laughing because of the pain." Everyone knew that life could be rich and fulfilling—unless, of course, you encountered some physical, psychological or spiritual misfortune. But a good way to deal with the worst in life is to laugh. Laughter is not only an expression of pleasure. It's also an expression of the truth of things, a recognition of how things really are.

A Few Quandaries

People have trouble believing that rheumatoid arthritis is a spiritual as well as physical illness. If I mention this, they quibble about it: "Oh, surely there's a spiritual trigger involved, but that's not the same as an underlying cause." Or, "Are you saying that rheumatoid arthritis is psychosomatic?"

On the whole, people who aren't rheumatoid—or who have RA confused with osteoarthritis—have considered themselves authorities on my experience. They had an aunt who . . . They had a great-uncle who . . . They are quick to recommend glucosamine, fish oil, locally grown remedies, hot showers, cold showers, lots more sleep, lots less sleep, more exercise, less exercise, you name it. How to explain? It's true, the symptoms are similar to those of osteoarthritis: joint pain and inflammation. But the remedies and diagnostic wisdom are better left to a rheumatologist or qualified arthritis counselor. Still, there's no lack of advice giving from just about everyone I meet.

In most cases the advice, however ill-timed or wrongheaded, is offered in a helpful spirit. What could be wrong with extending a helping hand or a bit of charitable advice to a person who limps, uses a cane, or walks with an awkward gait? Come to think of it, one person (who no doubt meant to be encouraging) told me she knew a woman who completely recovered from RA after the death of her spouse. I gave her a sidelong glance and decided she had not followed the remark

to its logical conclusion. ("And the remedy would be . . . ?")
When I told the story later to the members of my creative
writing group, their lively imaginations quickly constructed
scenarios for doing that terrible husband in.

I hope you take my point. The depths of the rheumatoid
arthritis experience are both spiritual and physical. And one
of the greatest spiritual challenges is learning to handle and
deflect—graciously, in a genuinely charitable spirit—the
barrage of well-intentioned helpfulness, even when it triggers
anger, annoyance, irritation and a general sense of the injustice of God.

If I'm supposed to be so spiritual, you find yourself saying
inwardly to yourself and to God, why is it so hard to fend off
these small annoyances, the solicitude of strangers, the well-
meant pseudo-medical opinions, the world that reacts to me
as rheumatoid, defining me by my illness and not by who I
want to be—who I really am? Sometimes this whole blessed
thing defeats me.

Then there's the media onslaught of (mostly) scientifically
documented advice. Here's a dilemma: One of my spiritual
practices is to avoid exposure to anxiety-triggering media.
But I almost always make an exception when the subject is
rheumatoid arthritis. Today on my AOL welcome screen I
found this headline: "The Link Between Rheumatoid Arthritis and Stress." The article read, "Getting the symptoms
of rheumatoid arthritis under control is an important step
toward stress relief. Lifestyle changes, such as eating a
healthy rheumatoid arthritis diet and managing your time
effectively, will help."

So far, so good. I felt good reading this because I was op-
erating by both principles. But then came a list of symptoms:

joint pain, muscle stiffness, fatigue, weight loss, low-grade fever. Painful, swollen, tender joints—hands, wrists, knees or neck. Sometimes on both sides of the body. (*Should I stop reading?* I wondered. *No*, I decided, and went on.) Morning stiffness, defined as joint stiffness that develops after long periods of sleeping or sitting and lasts at least sixty minutes and often up to several hours. (*But I know all this*, I thought. *Why am I still reading?*) The article, which was fairly brief, then listed once again the symptoms already mentioned: fatigue, loss of appetite, weight loss, mild fever, numbness and tingling in the hands. Final summary: "Some of the symptoms of rheumatoid arthritis may be similar to symptoms of other health conditions."

Wait a minute, I thought. *Rheumatoid arthritis isn't my only diagnosis. I have other autoimmunity problems. . . .* Suddenly my fevered imagination began to skyrocket out of control.

It was midafternoon. The house was unusually warm, even for Louisiana. I began to feel weak, fatigued, a little nauseated. Almost without thinking I lost touch with cheerfulness—with a self-forgetful, open-hearted spirit—and began to worry. Soon I went for the thermometer, which had been lying neglected for weeks, and checked my temperature. It was normal.

I know something about suggestibility in illness, the way doctors and nurses in training may develop the symptoms they're studying. Was I letting my imagination drive me into symptoms I didn't have, didn't want to have? What about the self-pity factor?

Don't dwell on it, I said inwardly. *Let it go.*

But another set of inward voices cried out like Job at the injustice of an illness that comes without warning, pins you in a chair when you mean to get up, messes up appointments, plans, errands, jaunts—all the happy times everyone looks forward to.

Spiritually, this is the danger point. Standing on the ledge, on a precipice between trusting God and not trusting him.

Bibles are great at moments like this. Fat little consoling volumes you open and hold in your lap until the painful moment or painful memory passes. Or maybe you don't even open your Bible. Maybe you just remember the Psalm that most reminds you of the God you know and love.

Then grace comes all at once, as unpredictably as pain: The Lord speaks his love into the universe, flooding hearts (mine, everyone's) with peace and forgiveness and letting his healing power descend into one small soul.

There are a great many obstacles in life. Illness is only one of them. But my confidence is that faith helps us transcend such obstacles. One of the ways to deal with any challenge, including illness, is to choose the best of what is set before us: the most satisfying and enjoyable aspects of life. To choose life, as we read in Deuteronomy. "I have set before you life and death, blessings and curses. Choose life so that you and your descendants may live, loving the LORD your God, obeying him, and holding fast to him; for that means life to you and length of days" (Deut 30:19-20 NRSV).

Transcending Illness: Pierre-Auguste Renoir

Recently I learned how the painter Pierre Auguste Renoir (1841–1919) dealt with illness. Even as he lost the use of his body he continued to paint, expressing his joy in the created world. The great painter wrote in his notebook, "I believe I am nearer to God by being humble before his splendor

(Nature); by accepting the role I have been given to play in life; by honoring this majesty without self-interest, and above all, without asking for anything, being confident that He who has created everything has forgotten nothing." Renoir's son Jean, a noted filmmaker, captured these and other reflections in the memoir *Renoir, My Father.*

Renoir contracted rheumatoid arthritis in 1898. He was fifty-seven years old and had been painting all his life. His hands became distorted. His joints were often inflamed, and the inflammation damaged his extremities and his joint tissue. The medical knowledge of the time was far less advanced than it is today, and though he took action as well as he knew how by moving to a warmer climate in France, the disease continued to weaken him.

Remembering Renoir in his later years, Jean wrote, "His hands were terribly deformed. His rheumatism had made the joints stiff and caused the thumbs to turn inward towards the palms, and the fingers to bend toward the wrists. Visitors who were unprepared for this could not take their eyes off his deformity. Though they did not dare to mention it, their reaction would be expressed by some phrase such as 'It isn't possible! With hands like that, how can he paint those pictures? There's some mystery somewhere.' The 'mystery' was Renoir himself."

Jean said further that his amazing father was shy and "never liked to give any sign of the emotion that overpowered him when he looked at flowers, women, or clouds." Renoir never lost that joy or his love of the beautiful. To the last he was able to grasp the brush and pay homage to his Creator. He believed there was enough unpleasantness in life. He would not add to people's burdens but would heighten their joy. Over his lifetime he produced six thousand works of art expressing the beauty of landscapes, ordinary domestic scenes, the feminine appeal, the wonder of the human body.

Renoir was born to a working-class family in Limoges, France. His gift of drawing and sketching became obvious while he was still a child, and his father apprenticed him to a porcelain maker where, among other duties, he painted on porcelain surfaces. Later, after moving with his family to Paris, Renoir received formal training and in his early twenties was already showing his work.

In his early life Renoir was caught up in the Impressionist movement. He was friends with many other Impressionist painters, Claude Monet among them. But later in life Renoir came to feel that Impressionism was no longer important to him. He returned to traditional painting. He valued the art of the past, but he was no theorist. "You must not come before Nature with theories," he wrote in his journal. "Nature throws you to the ground. It is . . . necessary to make sure that, simply for love of progress, we don't detach ourselves from the centuries before us. . . . So many marvelous discoveries have been made in the past hundred years that men seem to forget that others have lived before them."

Beauty Remains, but Pain Passes

On his blog, May 28, 2007, Paulo Coelho posted a reflection titled "Matisse and Renoir Meet":

> As a young man, the painter Henri Matisse used to pay a weekly visit to the great Renoir in his studio. When Renoir was afflicted by arthritis, Matisse began to visit him daily, taking him food, brushes, paints, but always

trying to persuade the master that he was working too hard and needed to rest a little.

One day, noticing that each brushstroke made Renoir cry out with pain, Matisse could contain himself no longer:

"Master, you have already created a vast and important body of work, why continue torturing yourself in this way?"

"Very simple," Renoir replied. "Beauty remains, but pain passes."

Jean Renoir tells of a moment late in his father's life when a doctor tried to encourage him to walk. Discovering how much effort it took, Renoir made a firm choice. "If I have to choose between walking and painting, I'd much rather paint."

According to Jean Renoir, his father "sat down and never got up again."

> From the moment he made this important decision, Renoir's life was a display of fireworks to the end. Although his palette became more and more austere, the most dazzling colors issued from it. It was as if all Renoir's love of the beauty of this life, which he could no longer enjoy physically, had gushed out of his whole, tortured being. He was radiant, in the true sense of the word, by which I meant that we felt there were rays emanating from his brush, as it caressed the canvas. He was freed from all theories, from all fears.

The Grace to Resist Self-Pity

When I reflect on the work of Renoir, afflicted by rheumatoid arthritis, I think about the value of self-expression, of giving of one's own joyful spirit to others as a way to transcend self-pity and pain. Renoir expressed his choice in terms of beauty. Perhaps that is the best philosophical language. Perhaps it was the only philosophical language he knew in which to frame his personal commitment to continue painting.

I feel a connection with Renoir. Like that remarkable artist, I myself contracted rheumatoid arthritis in my late fifties. I remember the day when I was suddenly enclosed in an envelope of pain. My hands, wrists, ankles and feet were engulfed by it. I had no idea what was happening, but I was able to telephone the doctor. I managed to get from my studio office to my car and drive, in spite of the discomfort, to the doctor's office. The doctor knew it was arthritis, though he was unable to say what kind. A shot of cortisone enabled me to get through the first attack.

Eventually, through a series of such attacks and under the care of a rheumatologist, I learned what my illness was and how I might be treated for it. Through the ensuing years I have instinctively continued to pursue the work I love (writing and speaking) and my own expression of Christian faith.

For me, work becomes a creative solution to the obstacle of illness. Physically I am hemmed in. But spiritually a depth remains within such confines. Moreover that depth is enhanced to the extent that I practice the creative life.

In my own case, rheumatoid arthritis has been a challenge. It has affected my joints and done damage to my hands and feet. However, I am grateful to have good, ongoing medical care and the freedom to continue my work as a writer, editor and speaker. Here is a poem I wrote to describe my illness and how it feels. I also wanted to suggest that

transcending illness is not just a matter of wanting or wishing
but a response to God's grace.

The pain is unpredictable.
It comes in a flash, without warning
Pouring it seems like quicksilver
From some unknown sky-place
Into my brain.
It is a shooting pain
Sharp as an ice cream headache
And it roots me to the spot.

It makes me say,
On the middle step,
When I am dressed for the occasion
And expected somewhere,
"Bill, if you don't mind,
You go ahead without me.
They'll be waiting for you.
Phone me when you get there.
I'll just rest here,
Quietly,
In the dark."

It makes you want to draw the blinds
Against the harsh light of things
And,
To be completely frank,
It makes you question
The way God has arranged things
Things like
Life and death.

Sickness and health
And rheumatoid arthritis.

But in an instant,
Quick as the pain itself
You remember Eden
Green and glowing
And just beyond it
Paradise
With every holy creature
Joyful and at peace.

That is what you may call
(if you like to give names to things)
a spirituality of rheumatoid arthritis.
It is the human spirit
fueled by grace
and rising up joyfully from the chair
to say,
oh yes, I did have a headache,
I was a bit unwell today
But I am well
In the grace of God
Well enough to withstand
Whatever the universe is dishing up today
And well enough to ask hard questions
Not to mention
Well enough to hold my Bible in my lap
Until the day of Resurrection.

Henri Matisse: Exuding Calm and Peace
Was Renoir an inspiration to Henri Matisse in his own han-

dling of illness? Many commentators have noticed that although Matisse (1869–1954) lived eighty-six years, surviving two world wars and many other upheavals, his painting always exuded calm and peace, featuring bright colors and a childlike sense of joy. They are consistent with his early discovery of the experience of painting, which he compared to entering paradise.

Late in his long life Matisse, in spite of being a celebrated painter, was troubled by illness and could no longer paint. Dealing with arthritis and the effects of a colonoscopy, he was confined to a wheelchair. Yet the last phase of his life was explosively creative as he taught himself to "paint with scissors." Assisted by others, Matisse worked in color, creating new paintings with cutouts. These works are as deeply admired as his earlier paintings in conventional media.

The Irish painter John Nolan, whose studio is in Dublin, celebrates Matisse in his painting titled "Still Life with Matisse." He explains his motivation this way:

> In this still life I portray Matisse's painting "La Danse 1909." The vase is inspired by his gouache cut-outs. When Matisse developed arthritis and could no longer paint, he started using sheets of precoloured paper with gouache. He cut the cut-outs to the shapes he desired. The delineations on the fruit bowl and wall are characteristic of Matisse's work.

Nolan attributes these words to Henri Matisse: "A pair of scissors is a . . . wonderful instrument. . . . Working with scissors in this paper is an occupation I can lose myself in. . . . Why didn't I think of it earlier?"

There's a childlike quality about Matisse. For him, even

illness was a creative challenge. His colors became a way to work through, to find a new way into the future. In some of my personal friendships I have seen that same childlike creativity at work.

Sister Janet, Facing Unexpected Pain

Soon after her sixty-sixth birthday I received a letter from Sister Janet Franklin, CSJ (Congregation of St. Joseph), who lives in Santa Fe. The creativity I remembered from earlier days was still at work. Once she had treasured her friendships like Matisse treasured his bright colors. Now she spoke about a busy summer of traveling, leading retreats, and visiting cousins and friends throughout the United States without a word of complaint about the high temperatures everyone suffered in summer 2010.

I liked Sister Janet's way of expressing things. "The phrase 'all is gift' comes to mind and I felt very lucky and fulfilled as I journeyed around, even took in a few days of fun in Branson, Missouri," she wrote. "I am very aware that others do not have the opportunities I have had; I never want to take these opportunities for granted. I send loads of gratitude to each of you as I celebrated my sixty-sixth birthday with your lovely cards, thoughts, and gifts."

Then Sister Janet gave some more challenging news: "Now I am facing some unexpected pain in my 'older' body and need some prayers to get me through the next few weeks. I have had steroid injections to ease the pain and swelling in my left foot; I have had to be booted with a foot and calf 'air cast' to stabilize a spontaneous metatarsal bone fracture, same foot, from walking wrong on it for so long. This to avoid surgery. The other thing is some gum receding, which requires a skin graft this week. So as I take all this in and ask for your prayers and strength, I can take a big look at it all and say hoof-and-mouth disease has come my way rather unexpectedly. A little humor helps, right?"

It was clear from the way she closed her letter that Sister Janet has put her faith in Christ. "May Christ in us be our healing and our strength, our daily encouragement," she wrote. "We walk by faith! I am praying for you."

Jim Forest, Moving into Dark Places

Jim Forest, a longtime associate of Dorothy Day's and a friend of Thomas Merton's, views the spiritual life from a special angle when he writes about his own illness and treatment. In *The Road to Emmaus* Forest sees the spiritual life as pilgrimage. This exploration soon moves into "dark places," and Forest quotes John of the Cross, saying, "If you wish to be sure of the road you are traveling, close your eyes and walk in the dark." Forest's theology is sound, for he connects anxiety and desolation to a spirituality of the cross.

One crucial stop on the journey takes us into Forest's own time of trial. He tells us that when he was diagnosed with kidney disease he resisted the onset of the illness and the possibility of dialysis. Now he has been in dialysis for many months. At first Forest avoided religious interpretation, seeing his illness as merely "rotten luck." But now he reports a change of heart: "What I had desperately hoped to avoid is now normal. I now spend nearly twelve hours a week—fifty hours a month, six hundred a year—at the dialysis clinic. Dialysis is part of the core structure of each week."

Forest says he has had to rethink how to use his drastically reduced work time. Who among us cannot on some

level identify with such loss, such diminishment? But Forest
has come to see a spiritual meaning here: "It finally dawned
on me that the hospital I dreaded visiting is actually holy
ground. My main pilgrimage these days is the unprayed-for
blessing of regularly going to a place where everyone is sick,
caring for the sick, or visiting the sick."

Through reflection Forest has connected the dependence
of the sick person with being poor in spirit. The sick person
is "by definition on the ladder of the Beatitudes. Each of us
may still have quite a lot of climbing to do, but, thanks to
illness, at least we've made a start. We are on the first rung."
At the end of a session of dialysis, Forest sometimes says to
the nurse, "Thanks for saving my life." The spiritual fruit of
his ordeal is gratitude.

Help and Healing

Here is a poem that Bill Vaswig included in one of his news-
letters. It comes from a book by William Barclay called
Prayers for Help and Healing. It helped me to understand, in
part, how Vaswig was able to transcend the pain and the
knowledge of his closeness to death.

For One Who Has Realized That He Is Growing Old

O God,
It seems like yesterday
     that I went out to work for the first time;
and now I haven't much longer to go,
     and I'm well over the half-way line.
I can't shut my eyes to the fact
     that I'm getting older.
Physically, I get more easily tired,

and any effort becomes more and more an effort.
Mentally, I'm slower;
  I can't work for so long a time;
    and concentration is more difficult.
First and foremost, help me to realize quite clearly
  what I can do and I can't do,
    and to accept my necessary limitations.
And then help me to be thankful
  for all that the years have given me,
    and for all the experience that life has
      brought to me.
Help me to use what is left to me of life
  wisely and well;
for time is short now,
  and I dare not waste any of it.

Let me remember what the prophet said,
  Your old men shall dream dreams,
  and your young men shall see visions.
                                    Joel 2:28

Long as my life shall last,
  Teach me thy way!
Where'er my lot be cast,
  Teach me thy way!
Until the race is run,
Until the journey done,
Until the crown is won,
  Teach me thy way!

What do we learn from these grateful lives? Principally that there is no answer to the great questions: illness, death, suffering, vulnerability. There is no answer but faith in Jesus

Christ. That is the gratitude that leads to the cross—and beyond it, to the crown.

Can We Be Happy?

Can we be happy when we are older—even very much older? Yes, of course. But there's a catch. We have to choose happiness. For some the later years are a return to faith and a moving beyond the immature faith that prays for worldly gifts to a kind of happiness that rests in God's grace.

Peter Bowles, the British actor, is a good example. His autobiography, written at age seventy-four, has an evocative title: *Ask Me If I'm Happy*. When this phrase first appears in the book the question seems to be a very worldly and secular one. It's all about getting paid a fair wage in a particular role. But by the end of the narrative, we see where Bowles's real happiness lies. In his later years he has been able to exercise his talent in ways he believes in. He is grateful for a long, faithful marriage, for friendship and the support of colleagues, and for the achievements of his later years. He also tells at least one story about answered prayer.

> Although I'm not a religious man, I was desperate. Three teenage children to feed, a stage career that had well and truly dried up, a decade or more of dead-end TV roles and a beautiful and talented wife who had given up her own acting ambitions to support me. I needed help, and I was going straight to the top to get it.
>
> Like many people, I will often go into a church to admire the architecture. But the one I chose that day was a modern, utilitarian building of no visual merit whatsoever.
>
> Although I have been known to offer up a prayer of

thanks for the many good things in my life, on this occasion, for the first and only time, I was in a church for the express purpose of seeking divine assistance. "Please help me," I prayed. "I am going mad."

Bowles was astonished when his prayer was answered and two acting assignments came to him right away. Never mind that he bungled them somewhat. His memoir is full of bunglings and also full of gratitude. In spite of occasional stalking and harassing encounters with troubled fans, Bowles enjoys his popularity with the British and American viewing public.

"I am very lucky," he writes. "I feel free to walk the streets, happy to take the tube and find that people near me greet me with a warm smile and a gratefully received compliment. These are the true fans, and I really treasure them."

Ask me if I'm happy, he says. And the answer is yes.

Expect to Be Happier

Andrew J. Oswald, a professor of psychology at Warwick Business School in England, has published several studies on human happiness and was recently quoted in the *New York Times* about his findings. "It's a very encouraging fact that we can expect to be happier in our early 80s than we were in our 20s," he said. "And it's not being driven predominantly by things that happen in life. It's something very deep and quite human that seems to be driving this."

The study in question was a large Gallup poll showing that "by almost any measure, people get happier as they get older, and researchers are not sure why." Arthur A. Stone, the lead author of a study based on the survey, said, "It could be that there are environmental changes . . . [or] it could be psychological changes about the way we view the world, or it could even be biological—for example brain chemistry or endocrine changes."

The telephone survey, carried out in 2008, was designed to evaluate "global well-being" by asking people to reflect on their personal happiness in a measurable, formalized way. More than 340,000 people aged eighteen to eighty-five were asked various questions about age, sex, current events, personal finances, health and other matters. Participants ranked their overall life satisfaction on a ten-point scale. Then they were asked, "Did you experience the following feelings during a large part of the day yesterday: enjoyment, happiness, stress, worry, anger, sadness?" The researchers felt these answers were more reliable, showing participants' immediate experience of those psychological states.

Published online in the proceedings of the National Academy of Sciences, the results were encouraging for those of us who are getting older and those who are already old. They contradicted the notion that old age is a harder time of life. In the study, people at age eighteen felt "pretty good about themselves." But then life began to depress them. They felt worse and worse until age fifty. Surprisingly, there came a sudden reversal at that point and people kept getting happier as they aged. By the time they turned eighty-five, they were even more satisfied with their lives than they had been at eighteen.

The study also reported a decline in stress as people age. "The researchers found that stress declines from age 22 onward, reaching its lowest point at 85," reads the *New York Times* article. "Worry stays fairly steady until 50, then sharply drops off. Anger decreases steadily from 18 on, and sadness rises to a peak at 50, declines to 73, then rises slightly again to 85. Enjoyment and happiness have similar curves: they both decrease gradually until we hit 50, rise steadily for the next 25 years, and then decline very slightly at the end, but they never again reach the low point of our early 50s."

Why a sudden reversal at age fifty? Dr. Stone, a professor of psychology at the State University of New York at Stony Brook, says the findings raise questions that need more study. "These results say there are distinctive patterns here," he says, "and it's worth some research effort to try to figure out what's going on."

The results of this early study say yes, we can be happy when we are older. And believers have a chance, through faith, at very deep friendship that uplifts and sustains them in the later years.

Reflections, Questions and a Prayer

In this chapter the author deals at length with rheumatoid arthritis, an ailment she tries to transcend through her faith in God and by various other stratagems. She also writes about the painters Pierre-Auguste Renoir and Henri Matisse, who also suffered from rheumatoid arthritis. Both artists were determined to remain joyful and to express the beauty of creation even in the midst of suffering. She also mentions her friend Sister Janet Franklin, who is suffering from illnesses associated with getting older but who also expresses a joyful disposition and gratitude in keeping with Christian faith.

What can we learn from this? Does a positive attitude help us live better and longer? Can we link these stories to the mystery of suffering and the experience of Jesus Christ?

Prayer

Lord, please make me grateful for good health and thankful, even when I am sick, for the gifts, talents and energy that remain. Help me to concentrate on recovery and to live with vitality within your boundaries.

4

Grief, Loss, Anger

Taking the Next Step

But the souls of the righteous are in the hand of God,
and no torment will ever touch them.
In the eyes of the foolish they seemed to have died,
and their departure was thought to be a disaster,
and their going from us to be their destruction;
but they are at peace.

Wisdom 3:1-3 NRSV

In the evening of life, we will be judged on love alone.

John of the Cross

*O*n my late mother's birthday, May 4, 2010, I got the following message via e-mail from my son Henry, who lives in New Orleans: "I am celebrating Helen's ninety-eighth today and starting to wonder what we should do for her centennial in 2012." (He, and all of us, called her "Helen." Sometimes we called her by her initials, "HRD.") I was glad she was so alive in his memory.

As the day wore on there was a flood of e-mails about

Helen from all three of my grown children, Lucy, Henry and
Sarah. They evoked a picture of her through her funniest
sayings. Lucy, who lives in Shreveport, Louisiana, wrote:

> So today is Helen's birthday and I was remembering
> some of her best quotes:
>
> • As independent as a hog on ice.
> • When you get somebody's number, keep it.
> • If it looks better on the hanger than it does on you,
>   leave it on the hanger.
> • No mariner ever distinguished herself on a smooth sea.
>
> Anybody else have any good ones?
> Love,
> Lucy

Our younger daughter Sarah suggested, "How about 'Did
you meet anyone you liked better than yourself?'" Sarah
also remembered that my mother often commented on
how nothing ever quite came out even, "just like biscuits
and syrup."

Then Henry chimed in again: "I always remember 'I knew
her when she was knee-high to a grasshopper' and 'a nickel's
worth of cat meat,' although I'm not sure the application of
that one." My husband Bill added his contribution: "Praise
from Sir Hubert is praise indeed!" About nine that evening, I
wrote the following to all of them:

> Hello, all,
>
> Dad and I really appreciated today's e-mail roundup of
> HRD sayings. The one I remembered at about noon
> today was "Count your blessings." She usually told me

this when I had counted everything in sight and felt I had no blessings to count. But after a few minutes, I would start counting and find I had quite a few. It was a glass half full/half empty kind of thing.

Love,
Mom

Count Your Blessings

Remembering my mother's vital, encouraging personality is one of the ways I cope with loss—not only with losing my mother herself but with every kind of diminishment. When I am up against the challenges of defeat, loss and failure, I find myself stranded in a patch of confusion. But finally a voice of some kind pushes through: "Count your blessings."

Why do I resist this time-tested, reliable advice? Do I think it's too corny and sentimental to be of value? Possibly. But when I set myself to count my blessings, I find that a complete reversal takes place. I must interpret all the events of my life in terms of God's love and grace. Instead of tallying up what I have lost, I gather my treasure, noticing what I have been given and what I have gained. It is a spiritual exercise, so simple it confounds me. But it requires a deep willingness I can't always summon up.

Setting Woody Allen's Ideas Aside

Recently the comedian and filmmaker Woody Allen was interviewed by the *New York Times*. In the interview Dave Itzkoff asked Allen about faith, which he said he couldn't relate to even though he knew it might help if he could. Then Itzkoff asked him about aging.

Q. How do you feel about the aging process?

A. Well, I'm against it [laughs]. I think it has nothing to recommend it. You don't gain any wisdom as the years go by. You fall apart, is what happens. People try and put a nice varnish on it, and say, well, you mellow. You come to understand life and accept things. But you'd trade all of that for being 35 again. I've experienced that thing where you wake up in the middle of the night and you start to think about your own mortality and envision it, and it gives you a little shiver. . . .

Q. Has getting older changed your work in any way? Do you see a certain wistfulness emerging in your later films?

A. No, it's too hit or miss. There's no rhyme or reason to anything that I do. It's whatever seems right at the time.

I was struck by the frankness of Allen's admission that faith might help him but that he just couldn't summon it up. I also noted how Allen's counsel of despair (funny though it might seem) contradicted centuries of Jewish and Christian wisdom—the wisdom my mother summed up in the short sentence "Count your blessings."

Dealing with Loss

The other evening my husband and I had a guest for dinner. This man was forty-four years old, young enough to be one of our children, and we found ourselves talking about the experience of getting older. Immediately we thought about the death of friends, especially close contemporaries. But to our friend we seemed to be talking about something fantastic and strange. He had lost relatives older than himself but no one from his own circle.

In a flood of memory I found myself thinking of close friends who had died. How I missed them. How they are present in my memory and imagination. How their vivid presence in my mind makes me believe they are still alive somewhere.

We often tell stories about friends and relations who have died. We do this not for their sake but for ours, to call them to mind and to remember how they blessed and loved us. Often we tell the funniest, cleverest things we can remember.

The wit of our friend Catherine Williams is always with me. I carry with me a thousand bright moments of knowing her, even though the best time was a brief eight years from 1962 to 1970 when we both lived in New York City and shared the fun of being young, married women. I recall how Catherine encouraged me to be a good cook by giving me an entire set of glass spice jars with fresh spices in them, each jar marked on the bottom with savvy culinary advice: "fennel—good with fish," "nutmeg—nice with custard" and other quick suggestions.

I once sat next to Catherine in a movie theater to screen *The Agony and the Ecstasy,* a film about Michelangelo. The opening scene showed the difficulty of carting a huge uncut stone through the city of Rome. "Isn't that always the way," Catherine drily observed, "when you want to deliver a parcel?"

She was physically handsome—tall and slender—and wonderfully well-spoken with a trace of her native Winnipeg and much more of her adopted city, London. She became the sister I never had, and our friendship continued throughout our lives, long after she and her husband John

Williams returned to Britain. Over the years we continued the friendship with visits and cards and phone calls. Her sudden death at age sixty came as a terrible shock to us and her wide circle of friends.

How did we deal with the loss? One way was by telling stories that would recover the best of her in our imagination. A second way was by staying in touch with others who remembered her—her husband John, other mutual friends in New York City and London, and her two remarkable daughters, Hannah and Victoria. They, too, told stories. We all called Catherine vividly to mind.

Several friends of ours who live in England decided to plant a tree in memory of her. Considering what Jeremiah says about trees planted by living water, I think it was a fine idea.

Mystery and Humbug

Actors, playwrights and novelists often give us great insight into the later years. Shakespeare's *King Lear* is the grandfather of this wisdom literature. In the play, Lear makes the colossal mistake of trying to buy his daughters' affections by leaving his property to them. He comes to the tragic realization that he has behaved like a fool.

Muriel Spark's comic novel about the later years is strikingly named *Memento Mori*, a Latin expression that more or less means "Remember you must die." In this brief and brittle novel Death comes calling by telephone, and the older folks who receive his phone calls are unnerved. They need to come to grips with the shortness of life remaining.

Recently an art film with Michael Caine took up this age-old theme. Caine plays an elderly magician who is a master of stunts and sleight of hand and who comes at the end of his life to an old age home where a lonely child is looking for comfort through spiritualism and the occult. Caine's character soon develops a warm friendship with the boy and entertains him out of his anxiety and fear of death.

One critic beautifully captured Caine's genius in the film: "What balances the movie is Mr. Caine's exceptional portrayal of old age as the accumulation of a lifetime's experience. In his performance the child, the youthful rogue and the forgetful codger all live at once." The film, *Is Anybody There*, is not exactly about religious faith. But it shows the importance of living fully and actively to the last, letting go of fears and childish anxieties about the life to come.

The Art and Soul of Grieving

In her book *Grieving with Grace*, Dolores R. Leckey shows how to let go of a beloved husband. In it she gives us an insight into the raw experience of grief, which is sometimes almost more than we can bear: "The question I framed a few years ago was this. How is it possible to realize a future of creativity filled with God's abundant love when my heart is broken?"

Leckey's book is not so much about her husband's death as about her own spiritual and emotional recovery, her letting go. She explains how her husband, Tom, who suffered from cardiac problems for years, went to the hospital on their forty-sixth wedding anniversary, not because of a cardiac event but because he had bronchitis and couldn't stop coughing. Tom was placed in intensive care, but Leckey fully expected he would come home the next day. At 5:30 the following morning, the telephone rang and Leckey learned that her husband was failing fast. He died not long after that call.

"At first it was overwhelming," Leckey recalls. "Alone I wept and groaned, sounds reminiscent of Irish keening. I struggled to get balance, some understanding of life in the present. Three old trustworthy aids came to me. One was writing, the others ritual and prayer. They wove in and out of each other."

Writing, ritual and prayer. These were the tools that Dolores Leckey used to reconnect with the experience of ordinary living. Through these routines she gained a new sense of meaning and purpose. She began to keep a journal, narrating the smallest events and reflections of each day. Here is her lovely entry for December 14, 2003—Feast of St. John of the Cross:

> This is an especially important day for me as I recall how, in his last years, Tom would quote the Carmelite saint: "In the evening of life only love matters." I brought a Christmas wreath to the cemetery today with the words of John of the Cross printed on a small card. I am reminded how indebted I am to John of the Cross, Teresa of Avila and all the Carmelites who through the centuries have shared the treasure of Carmelite spirituality, what I would call a practical (and poetic) mysticism.

How interesting, I thought, that when dealing with loss Dolores Leckey would turn to the Carmelites, especially John of the Cross. We know him most for his teaching of "the dark night," but both John and his older mentor Teresa of Avila were known for their joy in life, their sense of humor, their appreciation of spiritual friendship. Their intense prayer lives were rooted in love. John's spirituality is not about loss but about love, about clinging to God and no one else. But love is at the center of everything: "In the evening of life only love matters."

No Point in Regretting

In her book *Time to Be in Earnest*, P. D. James records a year of her life in the form of a diary, beginning with her seventy-seventh birthday and ending with her seventy-eighth. This is the journal that inspired Leckey in her recovery from grief and loss, although James wasn't writing about grief but rather the blessings of each day recorded over a year's time.

Much of what James writes is practical and ordinary, recording the events and tensions of each day. But sometimes there are moments of lovely reflection. "Youth is the time for certainties," she writes. "In old age we realize how little we can be sure of, how little we have learned, how little—perhaps—we have changed. Looking back on my life I do know myself to be greatly blessed. I have met with little malice and much encouragement and kindness. I am sustained by the magnificent irrationality of faith."

Now and then she counts her blessings: "I have two daughters who have been a joy to me since the days of their birth, sons-in-law whom I respect and greatly love, and five grandchildren whose doings are a source of continued interest and amazement. I go into old age with the companionship of loving friends even though we all know that we can't expect to travel the whole way together."

On one particular day James finds herself with a sense of unease, one that has lifted by the end of the day. Of this she writes, "There is no point in regretting any part of the past. The past can't now be altered, the future has yet to be lived, and consciously to experience every moment of the present is the only way to gain at least the illusion of immortality."

Yes, that's the principle we need to follow. But how? Memory is strong and seems to grow stronger with every passing day. Sometimes memory is a gift; sometimes it gets in our way. If we're not careful, memory can lead us into a painful review of the mistakes and sorrows of the past. Yet we know, as James reminds us, that the past cannot be altered. What can be altered is our attitude toward it. That attitude is part of our present and future and can liberate us from the painful self-reproach that bogs us down.

For me, the Christian understanding of grace is useful here. I'm thinking of what Augustine calls "prevenient grace," the grace that comes before and enables us. There's a Scripture phrase that captures it: "It is the LORD who goes before you. He will be with you; he will not fail you or forsake you. Do not fear or be dismayed" (Deut 31:8 NRSV).

Reflections, Questions and a Prayer

Consider how embitterment looks to others. In the film *As Good As It Gets*, Jack Nicholson portrays the character of Melvin as an embittered man. In fact, "the embittered man" has become this actor's signature. At one point Melvin throws an annoying dog down the refuse chute in his apartment house. What do you think about this temptation to embitterment? How can you guard against it? Is it a natural response to loss and disappointment? How can we let go of such bad behavior and move on?

In the case of those who have died, consider what kinds of ceremonies or rituals might help you to let them go. Does it help to visit and leave flowers or greenery at their graves?

What about asking for special prayer on All Saints or All Souls days? Should you plant a tree in honor of someone you love? What about having a small gathering of friends and sharing memories of the friendship?

Prayer
Lord, please help me learn to let go. Let me be inspired by your way of dealing with the loss of your own life. Help me to believe that life is everlasting. Give me a good sense of liveliness and humor in the later years.

5

The Sustaining
Grace of Friends

In old age they still produce fruit;
they are always green and full of sap.

Psalm 92:14 NRSV

To me, fair friend, you never can be old,
For as you were when first your eye I ey'd,
Such seems your beauty still.

Shakespeare

*G*od is full of surprises. One way he makes his love known to us is through another person. And we find it amazing to love and be loved. It's totally different from what we expected. We sense that this person has been sent to us: a husband, a wife, a sweetheart, a child, a pastor, a friend. "God sent you to me," we think. Or maybe the love we feel lies so deep we can't even express it.

Each time we experience love we learn how to love even more deeply. How to love this person. Or the next person. Or the next. Maybe we learn how to love again if we have forgotten how. The Greeks believed in three kinds of love. Well, maybe four. The Christians added a fourth—or did they? Was it there all along?

Storge, or affection, is the love of parent and child, of a family circle, the companionship that develops among buddies, clubs and teams. Do you notice how in families we develop a language of our own? Certain funny expressions, jokes that go way back? Nicknames, pet names? *Storge* is all about that.

Philia, or friendship, is close but not exclusive friendship. It extends to a wider circle.

Eros is the love of a man and a woman. This is an exclusive kind of love when two people are totally absorbed in each other.

Agape, or charity, is God's love for us, our love for God, our love of neighbor, the union that binds loving hearts together.

Our relationship to God is all about love. And the Bible gives us plenty of examples of how that love we call "friendship" may flower. Consider David and Jonathan:

> The soul of Jonathan was bound to the soul of David, and Jonathan loved him as his own soul. . . . Jonathan stripped himself of the robe that he was wearing, and gave it to David, and his armour, and even his sword and his bow and his belt. (1 Sam 18:1-4 NRSV)

Likewise, Paul and Timothy had an intense spiritual friendship, of which Paul wrote:

> I am grateful to God—whom I worship with a clear conscience, as my ancestors did—when I remember you constantly in my prayers night and day. Recalling your tears, I long to see you so that I may be filled with

joy. . . . For this reason I remind you to rekindle the gift of God that is within you through the laying on of my hands; for God did not give us a spirit of cowardice, but rather a spirit of power and of love and of self-discipline. (2 Tim 1:3-7 NRSV)

The prophets are both fiery and tender in their depiction of friendship between God and his people. In Isaiah 43:1 we read, "I have called you by name, you are mine" (NRSV). Hosea tells us how God lifts us up by his cheek:

When Israel was a child, I loved him,
    and out of Egypt I called my son. . . .

It was I who taught Ephraim to walk,
    I took them up in my arms;
    but they did not know that I healed them.
I led them with cords of human kindness,
    with bands of love.
I was to them like those
    who lift infants to their cheeks.
    I bent down to them and fed them. (Hos 11:1-4 NRSV)

Augustine of Hippo and his mother Monica also had a close spiritual bond. Augustine describes it:

Not long before the day on which she was to leave this life . . . we were talking alone together and our conversation was serene and joyful. . . . As the flame of love burned stronger and stronger in us and raised us higher towards the eternal God, our thoughts ranged over the whole compass of material things . . . up to the heavens themselves. Higher still we climbed. . . . And while we spoke of the eternal Wisdom, longing for it and straining for it with all the strength of our hearts, for one fleeting instant we reached out and touched it.

Jesus and Friendship

Between Jesus and his Father we see a very deep love and closeness. Jesus says, "For I know, Father, that you always hear me." This intimacy is union, connectedness, being with God all the time. I like to call it "clinging," as in that phrase from the psalm: "My soul clings close to you" (Ps 63:8). The Hebrew mystics called it *devekut*, a word that's hard to translate but comes into English in Bible translations as clinging, cleaving, sticking together, a mutual embrace.

Jesus speaks to his friends about the love he feels for them: "I call you friends, because I have made known to you everything that I learned from my Father" (Jn 15:15). "As the Father has loved me, so have I loved you. Remain in my love" (Jn 15:9).

John's Gospel describes the way Jesus pursued friendship. Today we might call this "hanging out."

The next day John again was standing with two of his disciples, and as he watched Jesus walk by, he exclaimed, "Look, here is the Lamb of God!" The two disciples heard him say this, and they followed Jesus. When Jesus turned and saw them following, he said to them, "What are you looking for?" They said to him "Rabbi" (which translated means Teacher), "where are you staying?" He said to them, "Come and see." They came and saw where he was staying, and they remained with him that day. It was about four o'clock in the afternoon. (Jn 1:35-39 NRSV)

One of the Christian writers who teaches me about Jesus is John of the Cross. John of the Cross enlightens me not only by his writings but by the way he lived. He was a little man, only four foot eleven, and he lived only forty-nine years—little Friar John. I especially cherish the story of John and the bricklayers. John of the Cross designed and oversaw the building of several monasteries. As the architect, the designer, he could have seen himself as being above his workers. But the story goes that when the workmen came to lay the bricks, he joined in with them.

I think the incarnation is like that. The Creator of the world wants to spend time with us, to join in the work we do of building up the world.

A Mother Hen and Her Chicks

Every page of the New Testament tells us about the deep friendship and love that Jesus feels for us. "Jerusalem, Jerusalem, the city that kills the prophets and stones those who are sent to it! How often have I desired to gather your children together as a hen gathers her brood under her wings, and you were not willing!" (Mt 23:37 NRSV).

Do we recognize Jesus? Even the disciples did not recognize him immediately after his resurrection. Mary Magdalene was at the door of the tomb, but she thought he was the gardener. "Please, they have taken away my Lord, and I do not know where they have laid him" (Jn 20:2). In many of his appearances after his resurrection, he was present, but people did not know him. "Who is that third one walking beside us?" asked the disciples on the Emmaus road. And then they could not believe that this stranger was so out of it he did not know what everyone in Jerusalem had been talking about. And they walked on, talking about the Scriptures. Later on they had to reconstruct the experience—why they should have known who he was. "Did not our hearts burn within us . . . on the road?" (Lk 24:32).

So we see that in some ways we are blind. We are unaware. The Lord is with us, but we don't fully comprehend it. What do we need to do in order to see him? We have to let go of a lot of our bad ideas, our narrow-minded attitudes. We have to stop saying to ourselves, "Well, the Lord is busy ruling the universe. Why would he make time for me?"

We are not in charge of how the Lord's love will be expressed to us. We have to leave a door open for grace. We need to forgive ourselves for the bad stuff we have done and the ways we have tried to negotiate with God about our sinfulness. We have to believe that we are forgiven. That if our hearts condemn us, God is greater than our hearts:

> Little children, let us love, not in word or speech, but in truth and action. And by this we will know that we are from the truth and will reassure our hearts before him whenever our hearts condemn us; for God is greater than our hearts, and he knows everything. (1 Jn 3:18-20 NRSV)

We choose to love others in Christ. Even people who are a pain in the neck to us. Not the nice people we know, but the ones who get on our nerves. There is a story about Therese of Liseux, who was called the Little Flower, that illustrates this love. Therese belonged to a religious community of women, and one woman there especially got on her nerves. Therese decided to single that person out and show her special attention, special affection. Therese died very young, and this annoying woman went to others in the community and said,

"You know, she was my special friend; she really cared for me."

When Jesus is our friend we will have the grace of endurance. There will be times of trial. We will not always have times of consolation. But we will always have the friendship of Jesus.

> I am the gate. Whoever enters by me will be saved, and will come in and go out and find pasture. . . . I came that they may have life, and have it abundantly. (Jn 10:9-10 NRSV)

> Listen! I am standing at the door, knocking; if you hear my voice and open the door, I will come in to you and eat with you, and you with me. To the one who conquers I will give a place with me on my throne, just as I myself conquered and sat down with my Father on his throne. (Rev 3:20-21 NRSV)

> Jesus doesn't change his mind. He doesn't blow hot and cold. We have mood swings. Jesus doesn't have mood swings. He is faithful. And he will lead us always to the Father. In whom there is no shadow of turning.

Reflections, Questions and a Prayer

Make a list of some of your friends and reflect on the way friendship sustains you. How do you pursue friendship? Do you write letters or e-mails to friends? Make plans for regular telephone calls? If your friends live nearby, how often do you spend time with them, and how much of this is one-on-one?

Are you involved in social networking—Facebook, Twitter and so forth? Do you find this helpful in developing and pursuing friendship?

Spiritual direction is a form of spiritual friendship. Do you have a spiritual director? Or have you considered training to become one?

Consider establishing a spiritual formation group. Renovaré, a Christian organization that teaches and promotes spiritual formation, has a fine method in place for starting such a group and maintaining it (see www.renovare.us). Consider using the Renovaré Life With God Bible, which offers interpretations of Bible texts in the light of spiritual formation and transformation.

Evaluate the groups you belong to in the light of friendship. Have some of these groups (more than others) put you in touch with like-minded souls?

Prayer
Lord, help me to practice friendship in the way you did, opening myself up to new relationships that may come my way. Help me to see your hand in my friendships and to cherish them.

6

RESETTING GOALS
AND PICKING UP THE PIECES

To every thing there is a season,
and a time to every purpose under the heaven.

Ecclesiastes 3:1 KJV

For age is opportunity no less
Than youth itself, though in another dress,
And as the evening twilight fades away
The sky is filled with stars, invisible by day.

Henry Wadsworth Longfellow

*W*here do we find good teachers of long life? One strong influence for me has been the work of Peter Drucker (1909–2005), who is known as the founder of modern management. Whether or not he founded modern management, he certainly elevated it as a legitimate subject of study, and his deep reflections on management as more art than science are broadly influential even in the twenty-first century.

I came across his book *The Effective Executive* when I was in my early thirties, working in a hectic New York advertising agency. Intimidated by pounding schedules and account executives with MBAs, I devoured the book and learned who I was and how I could effectively contribute. Also, Drucker's words and thoughts calmed and steadied me.

A remarkable theorist of business life and enterprise, Drucker lived to be ninety-five and died just a few days short of his ninety-sixth birthday. Himself a master teacher of effectiveness, he remained effective even in his later years.

In a tribute to Peter Drucker by David Maister I found a list of some of Drucker's major principles for effective living:

- Take a position on an issue and try to defend it with reason.

- Talk straight; don't be afraid to call it as you see it. Don't be afraid of the sweeping statement. Be thought-provoking even when wrong.

- Tell the truth as you see it. Don't be afraid to slaughter sacred cows.

- Read broadly—get your ideas from fresh perspectives.

- Forge your own mix of economics, psychology, politics, history, sociology.

- Keep finding new things to be passionate about.

- Write to communicate, not to impress.

- Keep trying to understand the world.

- Strive to be a well-read generalist.

- Never retire.

- Be serious but not scholarly.

- Be an individualist, not an organization man—you don't have to build a firm to make an impact on the world.

- Above all else, maintain integrity.

While these principles were primarily meant for people in the workplace, particularly managers and executives in corporate organizations, many are also pertinent to long life.

Of Peter Drucker's influence on him, Gayle Beebe, now a college president and author, writes, "During these early years I was given a copy of *The Effective Executive*, Drucker's timeless classic on the nature of leadership. I was mesmerized by the way Drucker provided a comprehensive view of the work of an executive. My experience with this book triggered my interest in studying with him, and over time I realized why he earned the title 'the father of modern management.'"

Drucker's style was prophetic. Throughout his life he created blockbuster works that opened up an understanding of modern life. His first book, *The End of Economic Man: The Origins of Totalitarianism* (1939), was commended by Winston Churchill and became required reading for new British officers. After the appearance of his second book, *The Future of Industrial Man* (1943), General Motors asked him to study its corporate structure. That two-year study put him in touch with GM's remarkable leader Alfred P. Sloan. The resulting book, *The Concept of the Corporation* (1945), revolutionized the world of management and launched the concept of management consulting.

What Drucker Taught Me Then

While Drucker is most known for his insights surrounding decision-making and managing for long-term and short-term objectives, for me *The Effective Executive* reigned supreme, with its guidance on how an individual could function effectively within an organization—without being swamped.

On my first reading of the book I found Drucker smashing my idols and helping me to redefine the categories by which I lived. One of these was the word "executive" itself. Executives, Drucker held, are not people who supervise the work of others. Executives are people who get things done, with or without support staff, often in pursuit of a long-range and sometimes elusive goal. On reading this I was at once able to see myself as an executive, though far down in the pecking order of a large organization. Even today I can see myself as an effective executive, one who works on behalf of a larger dream.

A second principle I gained from Drucker on first reading had to do with the use of time, always a sticking point in my daily affairs. Later, when I reflected on time from a Christian perspective, I saw time as not my own possession but as belonging to God and to be continually surrendered to God's reign. Though Drucker discusses time in a business context (Which projects will we drop? Which will we maintain?), he helps us see how precious time is, how it is in short supply and must be valued as the greatest resource.

I can't help noticing that Drucker, an acknowledged thought leader, did not write—at least in his early, groundbreaking volumes—about leadership. It was only later, and by others, that his work was brought under the heading of leadership. Dare I assume that this word was for him subject to arrogance and self-aggrandizement? Are Christian and religious thinkers quick to speak of "servant leadership" lest they think too much of themselves, becoming hungry for visibility and praise?

In the 1990s I wrote a volume on spirituality, business and enterprise. My first title for the book was *Cash Value*, a phrase taken from William James's comments on how beliefs make themselves known in action. But later the book was titled *The Reflective Executive*, and many saw this as homage to Peter Drucker. In fact, some of my chapters could readily be seen as commentaries on Drucker. I wrote about effectiveness, putting first things first, valuing time. I also wrote about ways to find meaning in loss and failure and, perhaps most important, seeing God as central, not governing part of our lives but the whole of our lives. Yet after decades of reading Drucker (in tandem with the Bible), I found I still had much to learn.

What Drucker Teaches Me Now

In later life, I find myself drawn to Drucker's ever-fresh, ever-green example. I find myself reflecting on his suggestions for living effectively and well. Though he himself was not consciously writing about long life, several of his stated principles are clearly relevant.

Never retire. Of course, this advice is controversial. "Never retire" was one of my mother's stated views, but then she was driven throughout her life not only by love of her work but also by economic necessity. Our cousin Joe Russell once told me that after hearing my mother advise him not to retire, he went back to Dallas and set everything in motion for his retirement. He wanted to get in a few good golf games while he was able to stay the course.

My mother's opinions about retirement were probably influenced by the sense of loss she observed in some people after retirement. They feared their lives were over, that they were out of the game and had no further way to contribute. "The gravy train has stopped running" was my grandfather's lament after retirement when he remembered the array of Christmas gifts he used to receive from suppliers. He felt stranded, useless, like a beached whale. This, of course, impelled my vigorous and opinionated mother, herself a business leader, to say one should never retire.

Broadly speaking, I agree with Drucker's counsel that one should "never retire." But I don't take this advice too literally. When the time comes for a person to leave an organization or an enterprise, he or she should leave. But that's only a limited form of retirement. What Drucker means, I think—and certainly what I mean—is that one should never retire from the enterprise of living deeply, effectively and well.

When I mentioned Drucker's advice, "Never retire," to a group of doctors' wives, I heard an entirely different view. Some whose husbands had been surgeons thought it was imperative for surgeons to retire to avoid the possibility of serious mistakes or errors. Others mentioned how grateful their husbands were for retirement. "I feel as though a great weight has been lifted," said one retiree who had often lain awake at night worrying about patients. Plus, wives are often grateful when their husbands retire because they can do things together, such as vacations and family visits, that were rushed or impractical until the retirement years.

Nevertheless, it is important for retirees to keep a sense of joy and purpose in living. They can join groups, take part in community affairs, continue to read and maintain an interest in current affairs.

Read broadly. Another one of Drucker's stated principles is to "read broadly—get your ideas from fresh perspectives." I have noticed how much Drucker's ideas of social and historical development were influenced by reading classical fiction. When he reached for a picture of the effects of the Industrial Revolution, especially the influence of railroads, he mentioned George Eliot's novel *Middlemarch*. When he wanted a reference point for the effects of industrialization on family life, he mentioned Charles Dickens's novel *Hard Times*.

Drucker's advice about reading broadly makes me happy with my own predilection for reading. Currently I'm reading *The Brothers Karamazov* with a women's group to which I belong. The reading is difficult—Dostoevsky can't be skimmed or scanned. And one finds nuggets of exquisite wisdom about the human condition buried in long stretches of dialogue. Yet this kind of reading fits perfectly with Drucker's belief that one must constantly seek to understand the world. *The Brothers Karamazov* is considered a great work of art by such as Sigmund Freud, Albert Einstein, Pope Benedict XVI and Eugene Peterson, to name just a few. High time that I in my later years join the ranks of Dostoevsky's readers.

Keep trying to understand the world. When Drucker suggests that we read broadly, he does not furnish a reading list. His idea is that we follow our own agendas, go where our vital intellectual curiosity leads. More than likely his own list would be too confining, and he knows it. Like the master teacher he is, he wants us to open ourselves to the full span of human experience, to ask the questions he may not have thought to ask.

When I talked with Gayle Beebe about his impressions of Drucker in his later years, he assured me that Drucker's vitality was a matter of continuing intellectual hunger, of on-going curiosity. One manifestation of this, I felt, was Drucker's capacity to philosophize and reflect on the future. Over his long lifetime he saw many changes in society. His enthusiasm for the free market and for free enterprise was all about human liberation and empowerment. Appalled by corporate manifestations of greed and soaring CEO compensation, he was something of an egalitarian. But he believed not only in corporations, not only in NGOs, but also in new technology which would reshape the world. He lived well into the information society and coined the term "knowledge worker," which neatly describes much of the work force today.

Above all else, maintain integrity. Very late in Drucker's life Gayle Beebe provided me with the *BusinessWeek* cover story called "The Man Who Invented Management." "Little more than six months ago," it began, "I was sitting within a foot of Peter F. Drucker's right ear—the one he could still hear from—in the living room of his modest home in Claremont, Calif. Even that close, I had to shout my questions to him, often eliciting a 'What?' rather than an answer. Yet when he absorbed my words, his mind remained vigorous even as his body was failing."

Wearing carpet slippers and socks too short, Drucker's mind still ranged broadly over ideas, social movements, centuries of human experience. In the *BusinessWeek* article, the interviewer remembered Drucker's flashy style of dress:

> Surely, Drucker never fit into the buttoned-down stereotype of a management consultant. He always favored bright colors: a bottle-green shirt, a knit tie, a royal blue jacket with a blue-on-blue shirt, or simply a woolen flannel shirt and tan trousers. Drucker always worked

from a home office filled with books and classical records on shelves that groaned under their weight. He
never had a secretary and usually handled the fax ma-
chine and answered the telephone himself.

Even for a major interview summing up his career, Drucker
found it hard to speak about his own legacy. While others
were calling him the inventor of modern management, the
management thinker of the century, Drucker himself was
"not in a mood to ponder his legacy." Asked about his own
contribution, he said, "I'm not very introspective," and
further, "I don't know." In the guttural accent of his native
Austria, he added, "What I would say is I helped a few good
people be effective in doing the right things."

I can't help appreciating this modesty. I think it is an
aspect of the integrity that Drucker valued so highly.

Get the right things done. This idea fits closely with the
notion of time as a limited resource, one that should be
managed with exquisite care. Both ideas apply directly to the
later years. Some people, as their lives unfold, try to repeat a
previous success. They remember the acclaim of the past
event and reach for it instinctively. But this way of thinking
and acting is counterproductive.

For example, my role as a grandmother is different from
my role as a mother. Grandmothers and mothers both possess
strength, but they apply it in different ways. Loving each
other, they do not compete but exert authority in tandem.
They act as a team to "get the right things done."

What I did well at forty may not be what I do best at sixty.
Or later. Now I have a new platform, a different vantage
point. I lighten my touch on the wheel. Experience tells me

I can exert very slight pressure—less and less—opening a way for others to follow. In order to express authority, I wait for the questions to come my way.

Following Drucker's insights, I build on the strengths of others. I choose to get the right things done. In Drucker's vision, effectiveness functions at every level. Leadership in its proper function permeates the whole organization, empowers the whole society.

A Patriarch Beginning to Fail

In commenting on Drucker's life and death, Gayle Beebe wrote the following:

> On November 11, 2005, I was walking down Seventh Avenue in Midtown Manhattan when I learned of his death. As I neared the ESPN Zone, the giant neon sign announced, "Peter Drucker, the father of modern management, is dead at the age of 95." He was just a week shy of his ninety-sixth birthday. We knew he was beginning to fail physically, but his intellectual capacity had seemed undimmed. Just as his life had begun at the start of the twentieth century, it had now ended as we were moving into an era he had anticipated and in many respects helped to define. During the twentieth century, he gave the world a new understanding of the work of leadership and the essential role it must play in managing the complexity of organizations that now define our modern era. He also gave us the gift of his life. What a century; what a life!

Peter Drucker seemed to confront life—even the end of life—with a concern for the future and the eagerness of a child.

Patriarchs and matriarchs look to the future. Abraham and Sarah left their home and went in search of a future they could barely imagine, one in which their descendants would be as numerous as the stars in the sky and the grains of sand. They went in hope. They exemplified leadership, integrity and humility. They listened to God's voice and kept their covenant with him.

The older we get, the greater our ambivalence about the future—that is, the things we will not live to see. But we reach earnestly to accept those limits, thinking of the future all the same.

Grappling with Retirement

When I reached retirement age, I struggled to understand the concept. Even while leading workshops on the subject, I tried to figure out whether retirement was a good thing, how it affected both parties in a marriage, whether to call myself "retired," "semi-retired" or, alternatively, "self-employed." I never intended to retire but rather to continue writing and consulting in a way that took account of physical change and adaptation. What is great about Drucker's principles (for the most part) is that they encourage us in later life. They remind us to continue reaching for a distant dream.

Does the spiritual life help us in this process of adaptation and setting priorities? I think it does. Getting out the notebook and making a list of objectives—monthly or yearly—is a habit often acquired during our working lives. We need to continue it.

However, there's another question that often arises late in life. Do I need to rebalance? Have I neglected my body, my health? Has sedentary living or the constant stress of commutation and imposed schedules deprived me of something important? Do I need more leisure? What will refresh my sense of purpose? Where do I begin?

For me, certain books and films have become a touchstone for this kind of self-reflection. I have mentioned a few in these pages. Following the careers of aging actors and actresses like Jack Nicholson and Meryl Streep has made it possible for me to encounter a certain depth and wisdom in life stories. I find meaning and a kind of encouragement in this. Bible passages also continue to sustain me, including those about Abraham and Sarah, and certain passages from the Prophets and the Psalms.

Back-to-School Night

Recently, on a hot day in August my daughter and I attended back-to-school night at the children's school. My daughter had had a hard day: impossible schedules, inconvenient timing, snarled traffic, missed cues, failed meeting times. But as we walked from room to room, the stress drained away. In the classrooms I found wisdom sayings and proverbs of every kind. Some were displayed on posters and signs hung on classroom walls. Others came from our exchanges with teachers, other parents and friends we met throughout the evening.

By the end of the evening I had captured it all on a three-by-five card. (Out of long habit, I always carry pen and paper.) The notes read: Pay attention. Something is better than nothing. Take the test. Show up. Don't lose your homework. Take care of the dogs; they love you. Be a caregiver, not just a care receiver. Don't blame yourself when you don't do everything right.

Scribbled somewhere on the card, possibly an after-thought, were the words "right as rain." It was the end of a long, hot summer, and with the cooling of the season we all welcomed a few sprinkles on the way home.

Reflections, Questions and a Prayer

Read the story of Jesus healing ten lepers in Luke 17:11-19. Dwell on this story and reflect on it. Are you like the one grateful leper who was healed and returned to give thanks? Or have you taken God's blessings for granted? Notice that Jesus says, "Your faith has made you whole." Then consider these questions:

What do I value?

Whom do I love?

Am I conscious of God's mercy and grace?

Am I grateful for the talents and gifts that remain to me?

Am I putting those to good use?

If I am not grateful, but surly and discouraged, can I pin-point the causes of this?

Can I refresh and renew and redesign my dreams?

What will allow me to dwell, not in the past, but in God's limitless present and future?

Prayer

Lord, give me a sense of purpose in my later years. Help me to change course when necessary and learn ways to contribute to the world. May I continue with whatever work you desire for me at this time, and may I enjoy the business of living well.

7

AGE

What's New About It?

Now I occupy my soul
and all my energy in his service;
I no longer tend the herd,
nor have I any other work
now that my every act is love.

John of the Cross, *The Spiritual Canticle*

But the autumn to a lover
Is the morning of the year.

Emilie Griffin, 1957

I have been following the work of Edward Petherbridge, the British actor, for years. He is a remarkable pantomime artist. He is an all-around theater person, actor, director, producer and costume artist. He is an innovator. And in his later years he is a blogger, publishing many of his rare photographs, production stills and some rather delightful poetry. One of the poems struck me because it offers a new way of looking at the later years:

Age, not youth, is the time of novelty.
One was always young, you see,
In shifting degrees, I grant you
But then the new thing happens.
One's leaves turn and will not green again. . . .
Walking on the thicker, lusher grass
I rejoice in this and know I've step by step
Never been as old as this or this.

Petherbridge is an imaginative thinker now in his middle seventies. He is raising some good questions. What's different about aging? What, if anything, is good about it? How can we appreciate the later years? Even though his own "green leaves" are drying up, he is "walking on the thicker, lusher grass" and he can "rejoice in this and know I've step by step / Never been as old as this or this." What a challenging, even optimistic way of looking at the later years. Something brand-new.

Facing Loss

Petherbridge is also honest about the way in old age we regret the loss of youth:

And then I see a pair of lovers
Who stop and kiss.
I remember that.
And adjust to a novel angle
My old hat.

As he reflects on his own long career Petherbridge examines the desire for fame, which is what drives many theater people and probably all career people when we are young and in middle life. Petherbridge tells a story about

Andy Warhol, who is famous for many things, including the idea that everyone gets "fifteen minutes of fame." (Of course, many of us never even get that much.) On the night Petherbridge spotted him in the audience, Warhol seemed utterly alone. Bereft. Petherbridge didn't want to change places with him at all. Such insight as this has to be classed as "wisdom literature." This actor has a sage and sophisticated way of reading experience. Petherbridge knows what others feel.

Petherbridge is not a religious man. In a blog posted in August 2010 he describes wakening to a radio broadcast of a Sunday morning service from Eton College Chapel:

> We were treated to some history of the beautiful chapel, the construction of which was halted when the College's founder Henry VI was deposed by Edward IV. Eton is presently host to a large number of choristers, forming a summer school, and they began with a Spanish motet sung so—ravishingly is probably not the word, and what the text of the motet was I forget and, of course, didn't follow in Spanish at the time—but "heavenly" style wins over content in such music. The sound was sacred and made one believe in . . . what?

Petherbridge wonders if the beauty of music is a clue to the existence of God. But the vision fades. It seems that the church has let him down. He's dubious about religious dialogue and practice. He's tired of God-talk. Yet he has the energy and the vision to see the later years as a chance for new beginnings.

Edward Petherbridge is expressing what Christians call "theodicy." One may believe in God but also question him, as Abraham did. But Petherbridge does not persevere, and the moment passes. However, in his weariness he remembers a childhood hymn, "Jesus Bids Us Shine," and offers a kind of prayer:

> Tired, I must go to bed, but I did promise myself to make a better job of those dark figures in the foreground of my pastel drawing first; it seems like a retreat into the cosy morality of the Sunday-school hymn I recall, "Jesus Bids Us Shine." What was it? "You in your small corner, / And I in mine."

Transcending Loss: Avery Dulles

Another remarkable man who used the later years well was Avery Dulles, a gifted Catholic theologian whose specialty was thinking about the nature and character of the church. The son of John Foster Dulles, secretary of state in the Eisenhower administration, Dulles was an agnostic in his college years at Harvard but had a decisive conversion experience and became a Catholic, then, after serving in the U.S. Navy, a Jesuit scholastic and later a priest.

The decisive moment of Dulles's conversion came about when he had been reading Augustine's *City of God* in Widener Library, then left to walk along the Charles River. On a gray February day in 1939, he noticed a young tree starting to bud. This small event became an epiphany. "The thought came to me suddenly, with all the strength and novelty of a revelation, that these little buds in their innocence and meekness followed a rule, a law of which I as yet knew nothing," he wrote. "That night, for the first time in years, I prayed."

Dulles's conversion in 1940, the year he graduated from Harvard, shocked his family and friends, he said, but he called it the best and most important decision of his life.

After a lifetime of influential writing, teaching and lecturing in such universities as Georgetown, Woodstock and the Gregorian, he became the Laurence J. McGinley professor at Fordham University in the Bronx in 1988, a post he held for twenty years. In 2001 he was named a cardinal, an honor conferred for his long years of outstanding work in theology. Since he was already past eighty, he could not vote and requested not to be named a bishop. Nevertheless he was an important presence among the American Catholic hierarchy in his last decade.

Dulles's health declined in his later years. He suffered from the effects of polio in his youth, losing the faculty of speech and experiencing impaired use of his arms. However, his mind remained clear and he continued to work and communicate by computer. On April 1, 2008, Cardinal Dulles presented his farewell address as McGinley professor of religion and society. The former president of Fordham University, Father Joseph O'Hare, S.J., was the cardinal's longtime friend and colleague. O'Hare read the address, in which Dulles talked about gratitude and suffering, drawing on the ideas of St. Paul about power being made perfect in weakness.

During the ceremony Father Joseph McShane, S.J., presented Dulles with the university's presidential medal. That same evening the cardinal's book *Church and Society: The Laurence J. McGinley Lectures, 1988-2007* was released. Some days later, on April 19, 2008, Pope Benedict XVI visited Cardinal Dulles in the Fordham infirmary during his apostolic trip to the United States. Again Dulles composed formal remarks that were given on his behalf. Dulles died on December 12, 2008.

I came to know Father Dulles in the 1980s after I told his conversion story in my book *Turning: Reflections on the Experience of Conversion* (Doubleday, 1980). I had acquired a battered copy of his fine book *Testimonial to Grace*, which was then out of print. This outstanding man found time to encourage me as a writer. We had several memorable conversations at conferences in Chicago, Boston and New Orleans. He wrote to me intermittently and sent a photograph when he was elevated to cardinal. Most amazingly, he once attended a workshop of mine and took notes! I offer that as proof of Dulles's genuine humility and intellectual curiosity.

Over his lifetime Dulles addressed many themes, but he will perhaps be best known for his ideas about the nature of the church, which he described in six ways: church as (1) institution, (2) mystical communion, (3) sacrament, (4) herald, (5) servant and (6) community of disciples. In his landmark work *Models of the Church*, Dulles explores all these roles, showing the strength and weakness of each model. He concludes by integrating each to form a more comprehensive model of church.

During the Second Vatican Council, Dulles was an important contributor and was considered rather progressive. In his later years he took on the challenge of correcting the excesses of the council and its interpreters, walking the straight and narrow in theology. Late in his life I heard him, at a conference, make an impassioned plea for Ignatius Loyola's principle of faithfulness: "thinking with the church."

In the obituary he wrote for the *Times of London* and posted on *First Things'* website, editor Joseph Bottum described Dulles as "one of the greatest thinkers in the modern Roman Catholic church and perhaps its most distinguished representative in the United States." He also listed the articles Dulles had published in his last decade. The titles show the breadth of his theological concerns. All of these efforts give evidence of a mind active to the last.

The Anxiety Handicap

A good deal of new scientific research has been published recently about how to be happy in the later years. One fairly consistent finding is that anxiety plagues us and slows us down, chipping away at our chances for happiness and joy.

You don't have to be an expert in psychology to recognize it. I'm not speaking of the clinical kind that requires treatment by a specialist, but the common garden variety. The kind of anxiety that crops up like a scrappy little dog constantly underfoot. Or like weeds in the garden that sprout up no matter how often we pull them. We could say anxiety is a nuisance, but it's really worse than that. Anxiety threatens to take over altogether.

Here is just a short list of things we can worry about: First of all, we can worry about being provided for. Have we earned enough? Are we saving enough? Have we managed our money well? Have we invested wisely? Have we planned adequately for the later years? Then we can worry about our family responsibilities. Do we have good relationships with our relatives, especially our grown children?

What about the things we own? Are we carrying enough insurance on our possessions? What about family heirlooms that can't be replaced, or land that's at risk because of environmental changes? What about earthquakes? Floods? Landslides? (I really believe that precious possessions should be insured so you don't have to worry about them.) Then there's health. Everyone regularly hears terrible stories about ill health, long periods of suffering that destroy built-up savings or tear families apart with anxiety.

Then we worry about ourselves—our track record. Have we lived up to our potential? Do we measure up to what other people expect from us, especially our parents or mentors? What kind of impression are we making? What do people think of us? Do they like us or respect us? What do they say about us when we're not there?

Are we achieving enough? Have we fallen behind on our inner timetable for success? Why is it that all of these other people seem to have accomplished more than we have? Why do they have bigger success stories or bigger swimming pools?

What about our friendships, our relationships? Is there anyone we're really close to? Can we communicate effectively with our children? Is our wife or husband really a friend? Do we have enemies? Are there people who are trying to undermine us—to hurt our reputation, to ace us out of honors and opportunities that are rightfully ours? Are there people who have it in for us?

What about the culture we live in? Have we done enough to make it better? Isn't it really going down the drain? What about cultural and social trends? What's happening to our young people? What about violence in our culture and in the media? What about moral decay among our national leaders and elected officials? Have we contributed enough to the transformation of society?

There may be legitimate issues here. But worry can take hold and make us ineffective in dealing with the issues. Anxieties may start small, but they can escalate readily. A habit of anxiety can take charge and begin to dominate our lives.

It's tempting to blame our anxiety on the nature of modern life, on the accelerating pace of things, on the explosion of technologies and populations. But if we read Scripture and Christian literature of the past, it's immediately clear that people have always been worried. And the wisest of them have learned how to put their trust in God.

How does our friendship with God strengthen us to deal with stress and anxiety? How does Jesus calm our fears and help us to move beyond worry and care?

Coping with Stress

New York City, where I lived and worked for many years, could legitimately be described as the stress box of the United States! There's the constant roar of traffic, the unceasing sense of conflict between people—taxi drivers shouting at pedestrians and pedestrians shouting back, people at counters shouting out their bagel orders, the constant clang and bustle of metropolitan life.

When I lived in New York and rode the subway, I would read my Bible, a small, leatherbound volume that fit into the wide pocket of my raincoat. I remember riding into Manhattan and praying but being careful not to lose myself in prayer—so I could stand back when the subway doors sprang open! In the midst of this, I began to notice that I was surrounded by a lifestyle of devotion. I was living in an old New York neighborhood that was gradually becoming populated by devout Jewish families. And they practiced a life of prayer.

Every Sabbath was kept holy and sacred. Families went together to temple dressed in their finest garb. On Friday evenings as they prepared for the Sabbath, the sound of their Hebrew prayers floated through the open windows. The women and young girls lighted the Sabbath candles and a hush came over the neighborhood, a sacred quiet as everyone gathered in the household for a quiet celebration of the presence of God.

The men and boys went up regularly to the synagogue to pray. As I came to know these families, I began to understand their faithfulness and devotion. Certain practices I had never understood, such as fasting, began to seem like something ordinary people do. On the doorways of my neighbors' homes was a *mezzuzah*, a small pocket containing a tiny copy of the Shema, part of the revelation given to Moses and the principal prayer of the Jews. The *mezzuzah* reminded each devout Jew as he or she went in and out to be at prayer, to be conscious of the everpresence and omnipresence of God.

I learned from my Jewish friends that as Christians who participate in the long Judeo-Christian tradition, we can gain the benefits of Sabbath by a more careful Sunday practice. We can also "make Sabbath" on another day of the week just by pausing, resting, setting work aside and relaxing into the presence of God.

Another aspect of my New York experience taught me a lifelong lesson. In the Jewishness of these neighbors of mine I saw the face of Jesus. And in a real exchange of friendship they taught me about Jesus as a man of God.

One family lived right across the street from us. They had seven children, all with Bible names. They invited all five of us to eat the Passover meal with them. The first time they did this, the first night of the Passover happened to coincide with the night we Christians celebrate as Holy Thursday. And the mother of the family said to me, "Be sure when you come that you tell the children this is the meal that Jesus ate with his disciples."

I was touched by that. Celebrating the Passover with this devout Jewish family allowed us to enter into the life of our Lord in a special way. We also saw that in addition to keeping the law, these neighbors of ours went beyond the law to help people, exactly as Jesus taught his followers to do. By a deep and personal grace I learned that I was living in a neighborhood soaked and drenched in prayer. I began to pray and to understand that when it comes to anxiety, Jesus is the best counselor.

Jesus Teaches Us to Calm Our Fears

Get beyond the idea that Jesus was a good guy who lived and died a long time ago. Think of him as very much alive and present with us right here—maybe even more present than when he was walking around in Palestine. And what makes him concerned enough to hang out with the likes of us? He wants us to know what his heavenly Father is like and how the reign of God actually works.

When Jesus is present to us, he makes the kingdom known to us—and we understand that we live in the loving presence of God. But in order to be blessed and sustained by this reality, we have to keep exposing ourselves to it until it becomes as natural to us as breathing. Jesus teaches us the fundamentals of spiritual transformation. If we will trust ourselves to these fundamental realities, we will become secure, safe from anxiety and spiritually transformed.

In other words, when Jesus tells us to ask God for things

we need, which he does, he doesn't want us to worry about whether God will grant the favor. He wants us to be cheerful, joyful, eager like children. This is an idea that is both new and old. Jesus teaches ancient wisdom in a fresh, new way.

The Spiritually Transformed Person

In the Sermon on the Mount, Jesus gives us a picture of the spiritually transformed person. What kind of person is this? He or she:

- does not worry
- is not driven by money and profit
- is nonviolent ("meek," peace-loving, a peacemaker)
- avoids hostility; is forgiving
- is generous to beggars and borrowers, not tightfisted
- does not practice piety for show
- does not swear

And by the way, when Jesus says the transformed person does not swear, he doesn't just mean what we usually think of—a person who doesn't curse. He means a person who doesn't have to use oaths to emphasize how honest he or she is. The person Jesus mentions is as good as her word. Her word is enough. The transformed person also:

- goes beyond conventional righteousness
- is righteous enough to be persecuted
- loves his or her enemies

What motivates such people? What makes them act this way? Can we think of anyone who is actually like this? Jesus, first of all. And the disciples, especially as they matured into a real and intense practice of faith. More recently in our own times, there are people who have been singled out because of their unusual righteousness or devotion, and we have glimpses of that kind of transformation:

- Pope John Paul II, who went to a prison in Rome to meet the man who had made an attempt on his life so he could forgive him

- Billy Graham and his wife Ruth, who made a tremendous effort and personal sacrifices for a worldwide Christian message

- Bishop Oscar Romero, who was assassinated at the altar by people who didn't appreciate his way of living out the gospel

- Dorothy Day, who showed solidarity with the poor

One spiritually transformed American within the living memory of some is Martin Luther King Jr., who took seriously the counsel of nonviolence. King was an eloquent African-American Baptist minister who led the civil rights movement in the United States from the mid-1950s until his death by assassination in 1968. Through his dynamic leadership, the movement was remarkably effective in removing racial barriers that had been firmly entrenched for many generations.

King rose to national prominence through the Southern Christian Leadership Conference, advocating love and nonviolent action. He insisted that such action was courageous and would work better than any violent protest. One signal triumph of this strategy was the massive March on Washington in 1963, which he led personally. A high point of this event was King's "I Have a Dream" speech, given on the steps of the Lincoln Memorial. King was awarded the Nobel Prize for Peace in 1964, and the U.S. Congress voted in 1986 to establish Martin Luther King Day, the third Monday in January, as a national holiday.

King's idea of God was active and personal; faith in God's guidance was essential. Vague notions such as "social progress" did not motivate him. Instead he was shaped by biblical stories, understanding God's prophetic work as on-going. King chose Jesus as his fundamental model for action. "It was the Sermon on the Mount," he wrote, "rather than a doctrine of passive resistance, that initially inspired the Ne-groes of Montgomery to dignified social action. It was Jesus of Nazareth that stirred the Negroes to protest with the cre-ative weapon of love." This is what King had to say about responding to violence with nonviolence:

> Along the way of life, someone must have sense enough and morality enough to cut off the chain of hate and evil. The greatest way to do that is through love. I be-lieve firmly that love is a transforming power that can lift a whole community to new horizons of fair play, good will, and justice.
>
> Love is our great instrument and our great weapon, and that alone. On January 30 my home was bombed. My wife and baby were there; I was attending a meeting. I first heard of the bombing at the meeting, when someone came to me and mentioned it, and I tried to accept it in a very calm manner. I first inquired about my wife and daughter; then after I found out that they were all right, I stopped in the midst of the meeting and spoke to the group, and urged them not to be panicky and not

to do anything about it because that was not the way.

I immediately came home and, on entering the front of the house, I noticed there were some five hundred to a thousand persons. I came in the house and looked it over and went back to see my wife and to see if the baby was all right, but as I stood in the back of the house, hundreds and hundreds of people were still gathering, and I saw there that violence was a possibility.

It was at that time that I went to the porch and tried to say to the people that we could not allow ourselves to be panicky. We could not allow ourselves to retaliate with any type of violence, but that we were still to confront the problem with love.

One statement that I made—and I believe it very firmly—was: "He who lives by the sword will perish by the sword." I urged people to continue to manifest love, and to continue to carry on the struggle with the same dignity and with the same discipline that we had started out with. I think at that time the people did decide to go home, things did get quiet, and it ended up with a great deal of calmness and a great deal of discipline, which I think our community should be proud of and which I was very proud to see because our people were determined not to retaliate with violence.

How Can We Become Spiritually Transformed?

What makes me a person who does not worry? Knowing that God is on my side, that he really loves and really acts on that love when I allow it. What keeps me from being driven by money and profit? I have to be secure and rest in God's love. Why in the world would I become a peacemaker? Because I know that God's love is enough: for people and for nations. I want to reconcile opposing viewpoints—without violence.

These characteristics are what Jesus told us to look for in a person who is living in the reign of God. They are not commandments. They are attitudes or habits of enlightened thought and action, ways of living that take over when we are in touch with the power of God. The Sermon on the Mount doesn't tell us what to do. It tells us what we will do when we have learned to be faithful to God's Word.

How will this faithful person act? She'll be generous to people who need something—beggars, borrowers, others who are stuck—because she knows how much God loves her. She's faithful to her spiritual life but she doesn't show off about it. She doesn't swear. This person goes beyond conventional righteousness. She lives her devotional life so completely that we know what holiness looks like. She's righteous enough to be persecuted.

Many good children are persecuted and bullied on the playground because other kids can't handle someone who is too good. These good kids get called names and made fun of. They may learn to disguise their good behavior in order to fit in or make life easier for themselves. Persecution isn't always a big thing, like setting fire to a church or bombing a synagogue or dumping garbage in someone's yard. There are smaller forms of harassment and teasing, such as backbiting and talking bad about you behind your back. The transformed person may actually provoke this by being the loving person that she is.

What in the world would make us love our enemies? And be kind to those who are spiteful? We love them out of the overflowing treasure of knowing how deeply we are loved.

That's the transformation love works in us. And transformation is what the spiritual life is all about.

How Do We Get There?

By way of encouragement, I would like you to remember this: No matter what church you grew up in, no matter what worship tradition you're following now, you are the heir to a powerful and wide-ranging living history of the power of God . . . people who have over time been spiritually transformed by their interaction with the living God.

And yet it is not enough simply to stay put inside one or more of these great Christian traditions. We need to actively embrace the love of God by living the disciplined life. If we begin to practice just one of the spiritual disciplines we'll find ourselves connected to all the rest. There are the inward disciplines of meditation, prayer, fasting and study; the outward disciplines of simplicity, solitude, submission and service; the corporate disciplines of confession, worship, guidance and celebration.

How do we grow through the practice of the disciplines? We grow in grace over time. That's why all the great spiritual teachers emphasize perseverance. Practice, practice, practice. In later years we may harvest the good effects of a long lifetime of spiritual formation, including prayer.

There are other ways to experience this transformation as well. I like to talk about transparency, a kind of clarified vision or way of seeing that Jesus meant for his followers to have. There is a sense of exaltation we experience now and then, very unpredictable but very real times of closeness to the Lord. We may have a sense of being caught up into his heart and into his life in surprising ways; sometimes it is so intense we want to pull back. I call that fear of heights.

Most of all, there is clinging to the Lord's strong and loving embrace. When we are praying people, we come to sense that we are loved. We live in the grace of God, the love of God. It's like Psalm 131 where we are the child in its mother's lap. We are safe; we are secure.

As we work along in spiritual development, we open ourselves to the influence of people who have been radically transformed by friendship with Jesus. They will show us what transformation is all about.

The thing is, each life situation is unique. We may never encounter a challenge of the gigantic proportions of the March on Washington or the Montgomery boycott. Not everybody is called to combat on D-Day. But there will be moments in every life when we are called to take risks for the gospel, to live what we believe:

- to intervene in a dispute between hostile factions

- to prevent an injustice from taking place

- to mend a broken relationship

- to make a dishonest set of circumstances known

Jesus is saying: The reign of God is here. The reign of God is at hand. You have only to accept God's reign and it will take over and transform your life.

And that is our release from anxiety. From worrying about being taller, or shorter, or having enough, or not having enough, or getting along, or getting ahead, or building a dynasty, or handing it down, or having success, or having our children attain success, or making sure that they have the right careers, and the right sort of friends . . . Of all that load of care and concern, God can release us into what we need most.

Beatitude. Blessedness. Happiness of the most profound sort. Because the reign of God is at hand.

The location is nearby, close at hand. Along the narrow way. Just over there. Beyond anxiety.

Reflections, Questions and a Prayer
Read the Sermon on the Mount (Mt 5–7). Then reflect on the picture given in this chapter of the spiritually transformed person who:

* does not worry

* is not driven by money and profit

* is nonviolent ("meek," peace-loving, a peacemaker)

* avoids hostility; is forgiving

* is generous to beggars and borrowers, not tightfisted

* does not practice piety for show

* does not swear (doesn't have to use oaths to emphasize honesty)

* goes beyond conventional righteousness

* is righteous enough to be persecuted

* loves his or her enemies

See if you can expand on the picture the author gives through your own biblical reflection. Name some individuals you know and admire who measure up to the picture of the spiritually transformed person.

Have you set aside regular times for prayer, spiritual reading or reflection? Do you give yourself permission for these things?

Have you made a list of some things that lift your spirits—things like music, concerts, plays, films, sports, activities, paintings, taking long country drives? How can you work these into your schedule more often?

How does "the spirit of giving" and concern for others inform your life?

Prayer

Lord, help me to listen to your teachings and apply them in my own life. Help me to know that being spiritually transformed is not a matter of trying hard but of relaxing into your generous grace.

8

FOLLOWING CHRIST

Where the Good Way Lies

Each of us is willed, each of us is loved,
each of us is necessary.

Benedict XVI

Suffering and diminishment are not the greatest of evils
but are normal ingredients in life, especially in old age.
They are to be expected as elements of a full human existence.

Avery Dulles, S.J.

*W*hen one of our friends pointed out that more than a third of American men in our age group were retired," Jimmy Carter wrote in *The Virtues of Aging*, "and that we could expect to live until we were eighty years old, I had one disturbing reaction. What was I going to do with the next twenty-five years?"

Carter expresses well the challenge of longevity in contemporary American life. Retirement for many people comes in the fifties. Carter was fifty-six when he and his wife Rosalynn left the White House. They moved from being at the top of American society to starting over again in an obscure part of Georgia with a heavy load of debt. Lacking advanced degrees, they could not teach. But soon they began to turn the situation around. Part of it came with what Carter called "a stroke of financial luck." A large agricultural firm bought their peanut business assets and several other peanut operations in Georgia. Also, Carter sold his memoirs for a high figure. The combined income wiped out their debt.

Later, in 1982, they established the Carter Center in Atlanta and became effective teachers and leaders. Essentially, the Carter Center is a nongovernmental organization working to advance human rights. But it also provided the former president and first lady with a platform from which to speak and work on behalf of many causes. Jimmy Carter has traveled extensively to conduct peace negotiations, observe elections and work for disease prevention and eradication in developing nations. He is active in the Habitat for Humanity project and he speaks out on the Israeli-Palestinian conflict. A gifted writer, he has published more than twenty-five books, including memoirs, fiction and works of political advocacy. Rosalynn Carter has devoted herself to many causes, including advocacy for mental health and issues affecting women and children.

A New Road to Retirement

Mind you, this financial and professional recovery wasn't established overnight. Rosalynn Carter struggled with anger and resentment. The pair disciplined themselves to live not with regret but in their own present and future. Jimmy Carter describes their experience and their trouble with letting go.

There were other reasons as well why moving back to Plains was not a pleasant experience. It was not easy to forget about the past, concentrate on the present, and overcome our fear of the future. It was natural for us to assume—like other retirees—that our productive lives were about over. Like many other involuntary retirees, we had to overcome our distress and make the best of the situation.

To pass the time, the Carters laid down a floor in their attic, got reacquainted with their rural property, took long bike rides and jogged through the countryside. But they were wrestling with strong feelings of regret and desolation.

We felt that nothing could replace the four more years I had anticipated spending as the nation's president. Rosalynn was especially bitter and angry, unable to accept with equanimity the result of the 1980 election. I tried to think of some positive aspects of our lives . . . but nothing I said or did could induce her to look to the future with any pleasure or confidence. For awhile we just paused and contemplated our lives.

Carter does us a favor in reliving these struggles. He shows us that even with faith such transitions are not easy. There is no doubt that both the Carters were people of strong Christian faith. Even so they had to struggle to regain balance in their lives. Part of it was a kind of disciplined waiting: waiting for the healing of their emotions, waiting for new activities to take hold. Rosalynn Carter also decided to write her autobiography. Slowly, as they began to work again, more positive attitudes developed. But still they did not yet know how they would spend their remaining years.

They were—in fits and starts—demonstrating and living out an active faith in God.

Gradually, through the Carter Center, the couple nego-
tiated the changes of their fifties and sixties. But a greater
challenge still lay ahead, namely, the challenge of perceiving
themselves as truly old. "As we entered our seventies," Carter
writes, "there was another potential threat to our happiness:
the forced realization that both of us fit almost any definition
of 'old age.'"

When they passed sixty-five, Jimmy and Rosalynn Carter
had to confront a new image of themselves. Former President Carter's analysis is excellent. The issue is not just the
graying hair, the spreading waistline. The issue is one's
own inward and personal perception of what it is to be old.
He points out that this self-definition is critical to allowing
us to live happily and well in the later years—as Carter
puts it, the "challenging but inevitable transition in our
lives" when we face reduced incomes and take on the title
of "senior citizens."

What needs to happen at this stage of life is an assessment
of the virtues of aging. What is good about being as old as
this? Instead of mourning our losses we should count our
gains. Carter was surprised when he wrote a book about the
virtues of aging to learn that few of his friends could find any
virtues at all. But to learn this positive turn of mind—and it
can be learned—is a vital spiritual and emotional resource,
leading to strength of character and high creative contribution.

Suffering and Loss
How do I feel about suffering and loss? Well, echoing Woody
Allen's comment about aging, I'm against it. But I know there is
a deeper reality at work here, a mystery I don't fully understand.

Jesus, himself a healer, a man of joy and friendship who

fully treasured and valued life, had to undergo suffering and death. And he accepted it. "Can you drink the cup that I drink of?" he asked. If I am genuinely following him, I need to drink of that cup.

Benedict XVI. Not long ago *Forbes* magazine named the ten most powerful people in the world. Among them was Pope Benedict XVI, a frail man in his eighties with spiritual, not temporal, authority. Nonetheless, his influence is immense.

The pope is attuned to a spirituality of the later years. In a visit to St. Peter's Residence in Vauxhall, England, in 2010, he spoke about how the growing number of older people is a blessing for society and suggested that caring for them is a "debt of gratitude." Everyone can learn, he said, from their experience and wisdom. He cited texts from the Bible: "Honor your father and your mother as the Lord your God commanded you" and linked that to a promise: "that your days may be prolonged, and that it may go well with you, in the land which the Lord your God gives you" (Ex 20:12).

Benedict speaks of old age with a certain sweetness: "Life is a unique gift, at every stage from conception until natural death, and it is God's alone to give and to take. One may enjoy good health in old age; but equally Christians should not be afraid to share in the suffering of Christ, if God wills that we struggle with infirmity." He spoke of his predecessor, the late Pope John Paul II, who suffered publicly during the last years of his life. Benedict spoke of John Paul's way of suffering in union with the Savior, mentioning also his cheerfulness and forbearance. "His final days were a remarkable and moving example to all of us who have to carry the burden of advancing years."

Benedict's comments about old age are convincing. He is, one might say, an insider. "In this sense, I come among you not only as a father, but also as a brother who knows well the joys and the struggles that come with age." He says that in our long years of life we can appreciate "both the beauty of God's greatest gift to us, the gift of life, as well as the fragility of the human spirit." We can "deepen our awareness of the mystery of Christ. . . . As the normal span of our lives increases, our physical capacities are often diminished; and yet these times may well be among the most spiritually fruitful years of our lives." It is time, he suggests, "to place all that we have personally been and done before the mercy and tenderness of God. This will surely be a great spiritual comfort and enable us to discover anew his love and goodness all the days of our life."

How do we appreciate the later years? We do everything we can to stay healthy, productive and cheerful. We find occupations that suit our new circumstances. We remember the best of the past, and we do not regret.

We cultivate a friendship with the Lord. Jesus bids us shine. He reminds us that, like Zacchaeus, we are children of Abraham.

We look for inspiration everywhere: in what is beautiful in nature and art, in stories past and present, in the lives of others.

We learn new things: how to blog, how to tweet, how to belong, realistically, to the present time.

But we dwell, most of all and however we can, in the presence of God. In him we live and move and have our being.

"Past all grasp God," says the poet Gerard Manley Hopkins.

For me, some of the phrases from his long poem "Wreck of the Deutschland" have become true prayer.

> I admire thee, master of the tides,
> Of the Yore-flood, of the year's fall;
> The recurb and the recovery of the gulf's sides,
> The girth of it and the wharf of it and the wall;
> Staunching, quenching ocean of a motionable mind;
> Ground of being, and granite of it: past all
> Grasp God, throned behind
> Death with a sovereignty that heeds but hides, bodes
> but abides.

My love of this poem has deepened since 2005, when Hurricane Katrina tore through my native state and made me question God's purposes, until at last my faith grew even stronger and able to leap over the most threatening obstacles.

Past all grasp God. Yes, that is true. When we trust the Lord completely we can walk with him faithfully into the future. We follow his path of wisdom, where the good way lies.

Father Val McInnes and the resurrection fern. Soon after he was diagnosed with a rare blood disease, and after he had received a sort of reprieve, Father Val McInnes, a Dominican priest in New Orleans, began to write his memoirs. He called the book *Resurrection Fern: Tales of a Dominican Friar.* The resurrection fern, which grows on the top of live oak branches in Louisiana and Alabama, became a symbol of life for him.

The resurrection fern, he explains in the book, flourishes in the wet season and dies in the dry season. However, as soon as the rains come again, the fern sprouts up with new vitality and life. Father McInnes says, "This plant is a symbol of death and resurrection; thus comes its name, the resurrection fern. But it is also a symbol of ever new life, since with each new rain, new life comes forth and prospers before it seems to die again."

To Father McInnes, this plant stands for the death and resurrection saga that occurs in everyone's life. He sees the fern as a "visible sign of the invisible spiritual realities that lie hidden in our daily lives." Through baptism and faith, he suggests, we are all grafted into the tree of life. Referencing another biblical figure, he adds, "And our faith springs up as living water inside of us—to life everlasting."

Even though his language is romantic, Father McInnes is a very practical man. He continued to resist and attempt to transcend the effects of disease. He tells one story of when he received his diagnosis at the Mayo Clinic with a very gloomy prediction about his chances of survival.

Next day we had an appointment with the hematologist. Further research and analysis revealed that I was suffering from a full blown case of myelodysplasia.

All the work-up examinations had been done in one day and we received the results the following morning. They were not too encouraging. In fact, the doctor said, "You have only three months to live." I immediately responded by saying, "You should never tell anybody when they're going to die because you do not know that." I pointed out that for twenty years I had taught medical ethics at Tulane Medical School and the very first principle we tried to pound into the heads of the new young students studying medicine was never to tell anyone when he's going to die because you do not know that.

My doctor was quick to respond apologetically, "I meant to say that there is no known cure." I replied, "I know what you meant to say but that's not what you said." He apologized and . . . began to review the medical options we had.

I admire Father Val's courage in dealing with his illness, along with his cheerfulness and charm. During his treatment at M.D. Anderson (closer to New Orleans than Mayo Clinic), he became a pastoral figure in the wards and managed to express his trust in God in many creative and warm exchanges. My husband and I worked with him as editors on the completion of his book, which details a long and productive life and much theological wisdom.

Where Does the Good Way Lie?

Every now and then the Lord seems to give me a new burst of grace. Sometimes it's a meeting with someone, sometimes it's a seemingly chance remark that gives me a sense of the nearness of God.

This time it was high summer. The temperature was close to 108. It had hovered there for quite a while, and all of us were praying for rain. I pulled into the gas station on my way to Shreveport for a hood check. The gas attendant was friendly as always. "Mighty hot," he said.

It's the usual topic of conversation about this time of year. "We had a drop yesterday," I told him.

"Must've been a little bitty drop," he replied, mopping his brow. "Rained just around your car? You must be a miracle lady."

"No, no," I said. "It rained all over the Kroger parking lot. It's only yards from here. Just a hop, skip and a jump. When

I went into the store, it was dry around my car, and when I came out, it was pooling up all around. I got my sneakers wet getting in on the driver's side."

I don't know why I gave him such a long explanation. Maybe I hardly believed it myself, the part about the rain. I could see he was still skeptical.

I thanked him when he snapped back the hood. "Glad I could be of service," he said. Then, after a little pause, "Sometimes I think that's what I do the best."

"Well, you know," I answered, "that's what Dr. King said. We're all in service."

His face lighted up. "That was a good saying," he said. "I tell that to people around here all the time."

We grinned. "Have a nice evening," I said and drove away.

Why did this encounter affect me so? At first it puzzled me. But on reflection, I began to understand the reasons it felt so powerful. First of all, there was the sense of kinship. Dr. King was part of his consciousness and mine, even though the service station man and I were not close friends, not people who usually spoke on an intimate level. Somehow the mere reference to Dr. King forged a bond. We were neighbors, brother and sister in a shared sense of meaning.

More puzzling but just as important was the rain that fell—seemingly just around my car. Those precious drops in a sizzling dry summer when the temperatures were skyrocketing seemed like an expression of grace. They were like the manna that fell just on schedule when the Israelites needed food. These few drops were like a promise that biblical things do happen. Yet I didn't voice this idea. It was the gas station man—as unexpected as an angel—who gave the interpretation. The drops of rain were miracle drops. "You must be a miracle lady," he had said.

There was still another sense of connection. "We're all in service," Dr. King had said. Just in the random filling of a gas tank on a miserably hot August day, God had surprised us with his Word. Each one of us had opened up a universe of meaning for the other because we had been willing to listen and to serve. We had ears to hear.

In an anxious world such encounters sustain us when we are able to reflect on them.

The Missing Eyeglasses

Overwork floods me with anxiety now and again. Once when I was hospitalized for stress and observation in a clinic, I was deprived of my eyeglasses. My son brought me a pair of drugstore spectacles, but they didn't fit. I couldn't read, and the only book I could contend with was my Bible. Actually, I don't think I could even read it. I just held on to the familiar, comforting volume and remembered the Bible passages so dear to me, retrieving them by memory.

Little time was allowed for quiet. But sometimes I could retreat to my room in the afternoon and watch the sunlight descending on a lone tree trunk outside. Each afternoon I watched the light descending on that tree trunk and saw the twilight arrive.

I also relished the dawn, which was my way of acknowledging Christ's sovereignty over the world. I was glad to learn (from the house rules) that rising time would be at five and breakfast would be available at seven.

But in spite of this the monastic spirit failed me. Solitude was frowned on. Silence was also suspect. Walking, long a spiritual discipline for me, was close to impossible because I could not go anywhere.

Love is a decision, I found myself saying inwardly. Then and there I wrote words that would later shape themselves into poetry.

> Here in this hole
> Of human habitation
> God is here still,
> No matter how I feel forgotten,
> I am a child of the light
> Christ my light
> Will come to my aid
> Wherever I am
> And he will not abandon me.

At one point the clinic gave me a brief window to return to my room unattended. They wouldn't allow me a pencil, but magic marker was okay. The wide bands of it were good. They fit with the fact that I had no eyeglasses. Still, somewhere within my dried-up heart was the nugget of who I am. The "me" that God would never abandon. Glorying in his presence, I wrote this poem. Oddly, this one also seemed to fall out of nowhere as a special grace.

> The light descendeth
> In a King James Version sort of way,
> Offering splendour with a "u"
> And colours
> Deep-dappling.
> God, being present
> All the time,

Letteth His sketchpad teeter
On one remarkable knee.
Then, pincheth the paper
As if to prevent
Twilight
Which even so,
In spite of everything,
Incheth and incheth.
Another day. Another work of art.

I tore the leaf from the newsprint pad and felt consoled. Sense of humor still in place, I thought. They can't take that away from me. And my faith is still strong.

I do not regard these brief episodes as flaws in my spiritual life. Instead I am grateful that my spiritual life continues to sustain me through difficult times.

The Plight of Other Patients

One of the most difficult things about being in the behavioral clinic was dealing with other patients there. Some were suffering from dementia. Others were delusional. One man who had me confused with someone else constantly assured me that I had been present when "Kate" was killed. No amount of denying this seemed to make a difference.

My son was visiting me when a male patient was receiving a visit from his wife, a local person. Just as soon as she left he assured us that he had to make a long-distance call to his wife in Texas. "But your wife was just here," we told him. He assured us that his wife never came to see him and he was worried about her.

They are all children of God, children of Abraham. But when people are losing their faculties it is easy to be afraid of them, and to be afraid of suffering the same difficulties ourselves.

I think the spiritual life offers us a new, or deeper, way of seeing. Our vision clears when we lay our burdens down and open ourselves to God's life, a life of beauty and love. When we stop, look and listen, our lives are simplified. These ancient principles work, but only when we are willing.

It's all about balance, simplicity and childlike trust. For me, one Bible verse says it all: "Be still and know that I am God" (Ps 46:10). Whenever I say this verse, I generally add these words: "Jesus Christ, yesterday, today and forever."

Learning from Jesus and the Birds of the Air

Where we live in Louisiana it is mostly green in October, with some leaves turning yellow and brown. Birds visit now and then and we love to watch them. "Look at the birds of the air," Jesus says. "They do not sow or reap or store away in barns, and yet your heavenly Father feeds them. Are you not much more valuable than they?" (Mt 6:26 NIV).

When our hearts are open we can learn from the birds, who do not sow or reap or store things up. Well, they do save string and whatever to build their nests, but I don't want to quibble with the gospel truth. The birds—and Jesus—are good teachers. They help us to be attentive, to stay balanced and still.

Even so, I also try to remember to get up and stretch into the way God has for me. The happiness my Lord desires for me. I need to stretch into the resurrected life, where the good way lies.

Reflections, Questions and a Prayer

In the film *Wild Strawberries*, an old man is traveling a distance to receive an award, and he reflects on his long years of life. Have you had flashbacks and extended memories of earlier episodes in your life? How did you handle them? Do you feel you have let go of regret? Do you experience the forgiveness of Jesus Christ for missed opportunities and failures?

Have you made plans for the end of your own life? Have you made a will? What about a souvenir list designating your possessions for certain people? Have you left copies of these documents with some responsible person, accountant or attorney?

What personal "unfinished business" do you have? Are you estranged from friends or relatives? What steps can you take to be reconciled?

Prayer

Lord, help me to enjoy the later years. Give me your guidance on planning and arranging things well. Open me up to reconciliation and show me what is best.

9

FOREVER,
JUST OVER THERE

Lead, Kindly Light, amidst th' encircling gloom,
Lead Thou me on!
The night is dark, and I am far from home,
Lead Thou me on!
Keep Thou my feet, I do not ask to see
The distant scene, one step enough for me.

John Henry Newman

When you face trials of any kind,
consider it nothing but joy.

James 1:2 (paraphrase)

*O*ld age is the new rage," wrote Herbert Stein in *Slate* magazine as long ago as 1998. Because of the trendiness of old age, he had decided to re-read Cicero's essay "De Senectute."

The last time I read it was 68 years ago. I read it then in Latin. Today I read it in the wonderful Loeb Classic Library edition, with the Latin on the left page and the English on the right. I read the right page. I can hardly believe that I read it in Latin when I was a junior in high school. And I can't imagine what I learned about old age, reading it in my teens. We didn't read "*De Senectute*" to learn about old age. My Latin teacher believed that reading Latin—any Latin—made tiny grooves in your brain that increased your general intelligence—not just your capacity to read Latin.

If I am doing the math correctly, Herbert Stein was well over eighty for his second reading of "De Senectute."

Cicero wrote the essay when he was sixty-two years old in 44 B.C. Following the custom of the time, he wrote it as a dialogue in which the main character was Cato the Elder and the year was 150 B.C., when Cato was eighty-four years old. (In fact, Cicero did not live to be old. The year after he wrote the essay he was assassinated by henchmen of Octavian—who comes into the Bible as Caesar Augustus.)

The essay describes Cato responding to questions from two younger men, one thirty-five and one thirty-six years of age. They ask him on what principles they can bear the weight of the later years. Cato responds with four ways that old age appears to be unhappy. First, it takes us away from active pursuits. Second, the body declines. Third, aging robs us of all physical pleasures. And fourth, it brings us closer to death. Cato then explores these four concerns.

Reaping What You Sow

Almost all of Cato's answers can be summed up by noting that people prepare for the later years by the way they live in their early and middle years. The obvious issue is health and bodily strength. Cicero believed in moderation in food and drink. All the ancients recognized the importance of exercise.

Another valuable asset for old age is friendship. Cicero has Cato say, "I have always had my close companions." Cato was instrumental when he was thirty years old in establishing certain clubs in Rome, "and therefore I used to dine with these companions—in an altogether moderate way, yet with a certain ardor appropriate to my age, which, as time goes on, daily mitigates my zest for every pleasure." When Cato says friendship "mitigates" his zest for pleasure, I think he means that such virtuous relationships regulate his desires.

Being a Stoic, Cicero-Cato does not set any great importance in sensual pleasure. And so being free of sexuality and its demands is one of the advantages of old age. (Twenty-first century, take note.) Instead, Cicero's Cato praises the intellectual and aesthetic pleasures an old man can still enjoy. But these pleasures are the fruit of a lifetime. To understand art, science and the beauty of nature in old age requires some prior commitment.

Writing about these things, the *Slate* author remembers Genesis 24:1: "And Abraham was old, and well stricken in age: and the LORD had blessed Abraham in all things" (KJV). Abraham was blessed because he had lived well in his own eyes and in the eyes of God. Stein updates this: Abraham has paid his dues. That is another way one can enjoy old age: to conduct yourself in earlier years so you can feel you've paid your dues.

On the final question of how to prepare for death, Cicero is only marginally helpful. Death, he suggests, brings release from trouble and the demands of the appetites. Maybe something better lies beyond, but Cicero is not sure. Cicero was still mourning the death of his daughter Tullia, and he found no philosophy to prepare him for that.

Old Women, Wearing Purple

There is a great desire to do something different, something daring, in the later years. The poet Jenny Joseph describes it in a much-loved poem titled "Warning":

> When I am an old woman I shall wear purple
> With a red hat which doesn't go, and doesn't suit me.

Joseph here speaks of cutting loose from her past life, of breaking out in some way. In fact, the red hat of her poem inspired the foundation of the Red Hat Society, a group for people fifty years of age and older who want to celebrate life. Their red hats may not flatter them, but they certainly suit them. The poem and the society have given a new flourish to the red hat, which previously was associated mostly with Roman Catholic cardinals.

A similar note is struck in T. S. Eliot's "The Love Song of J. Alfred Prufrock." In the poem Prufrock fears that he is growing old. He wonders if he should adapt certain affectations of old age, wearing his trousers "rolled" and taking walks on the beach. He wonders if he should part his hair differently and if he dares to eat a peach. He speculates that though he has heard the mermaids singing, they will not sing to him.

Joseph's "Warning" and Eliot's "Prufrock" are very different poems. But they have some themes in common. Both express a yearning, late in life, to be relieved of the constraints of middle-class responsibility: paying rent, paying bills, having meals on time. In this sense the poets capture a powerful idea—that old age should not be spent on regret. Ideally one needs to live fully and well at every stage of the life journey in order to take pleasure in achievement at the last. But one can still enjoy the fruits of a long life even without earlier success by entering fully into that life. By daring to eat a peach. And by making the journey, as John Henry Newman suggests, step by step: "one step enough for me."

Sarah's Loyalty, God's Loyalty

Loyalty is a fundamental value in our lives, whatever our age. The idea of *berit*, or covenant, is intrinsic to traditional Judaism and to Christianity. The Hebrews have a covenant with God that entails rights and obligations on both sides. The people have obligations to God, and God has obligations to them. The terms of this agreement developed and were more clearly revealed over time, until the time of the giving of the law through Moses. Abram is referred to as a Hebrew (*Ivri*) possibly because he was descended from Eber or because he came from the "other side" (*eber*) of the Euphrates River.

One tale about Sarah concerns her willingness to pretend to be Abraham's sister while they were in Egypt. She did this to protect him. Sarah, whose name means "princess" in Hebrew, was not only Abraham's wife but also his relative, either his half-sister or his niece. She became his wife before they left Ur of the Chaldees on the journey to Haran, and from there to Canaan. Sarah (originally "Sarai") was the first of four biblical matriarchs. The others were Rebecca, Leah and Rachel.

Sarah was unusually beautiful, which caused complications. When she and Abraham arrived in Egypt during the famine, Abraham reported that Sarah was his sister and got her to conspire in the deception. He was afraid of being killed on her account. At first the deception worked well. Pharaoh took Sarah into his harem and gave gifts to her "brother" Abraham. But then the Lord afflicted Pharaoh's household with plagues. Pharaoh knew something was wrong and eventually learned that Sarah was Abraham's wife. When the truth came out, Pharaoh returned Sarah to Abraham and sent them both away, though he showered them with gifts.

Later Abraham and Sarah traveled to the territory of Abimelech, the ruler of Gerar near Gaza. The same thing happened again. When Sarah was passed off as Abraham's sister, Abimelech wanted her in his household. But he handed Sarah back after learning the truth from God in a dream. (One of the Dead Sea Scrolls found in 1948 provides a gloss on these stories, by dwelling on Sarah's beauty.)

Another story involves Sarah's concern that Abraham should father a child. She was growing old and thought she was unable to conceive. Abraham was growing old as well. So she offered her maidservant, Hagar, to cohabit with Abraham. We may be shocked to hear it now, but this was a common practice in the region in their day. Tradition holds that Hagar was a daughter of Pharaoh given to Abraham during his travels in Egypt. She bore Abraham a son, Ishmael, who, according to both Muslim and Jewish tradition, is the ancestor of the Arabs (see Gen 16). This remarkable event is a kind of testimony to Sarah's misguided but fervent loyalty and devotion to her husband. This mutual loyalty continued over their lifetime. And as for their relationship to God, they received many signs of God's love and loyalty to them—including their son Isaac.

The Restless Heart of Orson Bean
Sometimes defeat is an entry point for grace. Recently I

stumbled across a story that illustrates this. It's about an entertainer named Orson Bean, who at age eighty-one fearlessly declared on national radio that he had become a Christian.

In the account Bean described his recovery from alcohol addiction. At an AA meeting he heard a speaker named Bobby, a tough guy who impressed him. After the meeting he ran after Bobby and demanded some advice. "I told him about how I had a few months clean and sober and about my reluctance to think about my higher power as God," Bean said. "What advice did he have?"

"Get down on your knees," Bobby told Bean, "and thank God every morning. Then, do it again at night."

"But I don't think I believe in God," Bean replied.

"It doesn't matter," he said. "Just do it."

"Why do I have to get down on my knees?"

"He likes it," said Bobby. And that's all he had to say. He stood looking at Bean for a moment, and after Bean thanked Bobby, he left. Bean was living in those days in a little flat in Venice with a Murphy bed. His story continues:

> That night, when it was time for me to go to sleep, I got down on my knees beside the Murphy bed, feeling like a complete fool, and spoke out loud. "If there's anybody there," I said, "thank you for the day." I had finally decided, I suppose, that since all else had failed, I would follow the instructions. That night, I slept like a log and in the morning I got down on my knees again and said, "If there's anybody there, thank you for my night's sleep."
>
> I kept doing this, day after day, and without my even being aware of it, it stopped feeling foolish to me. It started to feel good, in fact. After a while, I began to sense

that my prayers were being heard. I didn't know by who or what, but it was a good feeling. Then, before I knew it, I felt as if there was Something or Someone there who knew me and cared about me. Actually loved me.

"All right," I told myself. "I'll call it God. Thank you, God." And I really meant it. That's how it began for me and my life has kept on getting better ever since. Truly better . . . I don't know anyone who doesn't have an empty spot at the center of him, which must be filled in order to be really happy. That spot, like it or not, is reserved for God.

Perseverance and John Henry Newman

One of the most illuminating writers I have ever read is John Henry Newman (1801–1890). He has touched my heart in many ways. Newman, who lived to be eighty-nine, spent much of his life pursuing religious controversy. He was much like Augustine in that many of his ideas were forged on the anvil of debate. Newman was a wonderfully creative man who wrote poetry, fiction, theology, sermons, tracts of many kinds, letters and hymns, and he was a leading figure in English Christianity during his lifetime.

In his youth Newman was educated at Oxford University, ordained an Anglican priest, and pursued a brilliant time of preaching and leadership in Oxford. He was important in the Tractarian movement, sometimes called the Oxford Movement, in which many Anglicans revived aspects of Roman Catholic teaching and practice.

Needing a period of discernment, Newman left Oxford in 1842 to found a faith community at Littlemore, not far away. There he lived under something like monastic conditions with a small band of followers. Buildings were adapted in what is now College Lane, Littlemore, opposite the inn. The construction work on this "Anglican monastery" involved stables, a granary and buildings for stagecoaches. Littlemore attracted publicity and curiosity in Oxford, along with a certain amount of sarcasm and criticism, which Newman tried to downplay.

Newman got some of his disciples to write the lives of the English saints, while he spent his own time completing his *Essay on the Development of Christian Doctrine*. In February 1843 he published, as an advertisement in the *Oxford Conservative Journal*, an anonymous retraction of hard things he had said against Rome. In September 1843, Newman preached his last Anglican sermon at Littlemore and resigned the living. An interval of two years passed before Newman was received into the Roman Catholic Church in 1845. The personal consequences were great.

For a long time Newman had been controversial because he sought to Romanize the Anglican church. When he became a Roman Catholic he was constantly criticized both by Anglicans and Protestants who thought him far too subtle and dishonest, and by Roman Catholics who mistrusted his change of allegiance. Nevertheless Newman persevered and was known for founding the Oratorians, a community of Catholic priests who dedicated themselves to prayer and service in Birmingham, England, and in London.

For twenty years Newman suffered false allegations from those in Rome who were fearful of his teaching and his character. Some former friends, influential Roman Catholics, out of spite and jealousy had made him look bad with Pius IX. But after the pope's death in February 1878, Newman came into favor in Rome once again. By coincidence, in that same month Newman returned to his dear Oxford as an honorary fellow of Trinity College.

Despite his troubles with Rome, Newman had many admirers on British soil who lobbied on his behalf. The new pope, Leo XIII, was already considering how to honor the distinguished and aged Oratorian. In February 1879, Pope Leo announced his intent to bestow on Newman the cardinal's hat. The message affected Newman to tears. He said the cloud was lifted from him forever.

The press was hungry for news in Newman's day just as it is in ours. A rumor that Newman had declined the purple made its way to the press and nearly destroyed his chances. But Newman, frail and elderly, made the physically hard journey to Rome, where he was named cardinal-deacon of the title of St. George on May 12, 1879. In his acceptance speech, he set the record straight and responded to many of his critics. A century ahead of Jenny Joseph's poem, as an old man he wore purple, as well as a red hat!

Lacking any official duties, Newman devoted his last years to revising and completing his own writings, which are surely his greatest contribution. (When living on a scanty income and scarcely able to buy food, the novelist and poet Muriel Spark bought thirteen volumes of Newman's writings!)

Today Newman's life is seen in some quarters as a kind of reconciliation between Rome and Canterbury. The Holy See would certainly want it viewed that way. Death came with little suffering, on August 11, 1890. Newman's funeral was a great public event. He lies in the same grave with his spiritual brother Ambrose St. John, whom he called his "life under

God for thirty-two years." His motto as cardinal, taken from St. Francis de Sales, was *cor ad cor loquitur* ("heart speaks to heart"); it hints at the secret of Newman's eloquence, his way of piercing the soul. On his epitaph we read, *Ex umbris et imaginibus in veritatem* ("From shadows and symbols toward truth"), a theme that goes back to Plato's *Republic*.

A gifted writer, Newman embodied much of his own dear Oxford. He was a deeply educated man who used his talents well. From Cicero he gained a lucid style, from the Greek tragedians a power of expression, from the church fathers a preference for personal teaching, and from Shakespeare and Hooker (to name only two) a fine sense of the English language. One of his notable works, *The Idea of a University*, raised a high ideal for education. Newman's advocacy helped on many levels to secure rights for Roman Catholics and a greater tolerance of them. During a recent visit of Pope Benedict XVI to Britain, Newman was beatified and will no doubt ultimately be declared a saint.

For all his celebrity, I think Newman was essentially a lonely man, taking comfort in his books, his papers and his friendship with God. His passionate commitment to the Almighty was the saving grace of a long life, as one of his famous prayers illustrates:

> God has appointed me
> To do him some definite service.
> He has committed some work to me
> That he has not committed to another.
> I shall do good. I shall do his work.

This prayer also frames Newman's anguish at being "thrown among strangers." Many converts to Catholicism experience this sense of dislocation. It is true that Newman spent much of his life in alien territory, making a statement for truth that others could not hear. Newman's life to the end was about submission and surrender. He was led by a kindly light amid the encircling gloom.

Abraham's Death

The Bible records the death of Abraham. He gave all that he had to Isaac. But he also gave gifts to the sons of his concubines, and while he was still living he sent them eastward, away from Isaac. According to Genesis 25:7 he lived one hundred and seventy-five years: "Then Abraham breathed his last and died in a good old age, an old man and full of years, and was gathered to his people. And his sons Isaac and Ishmael buried him in the cave of Machpelah, which is before Mamre, in the field of Ephron the son of Zohar the Hittite, the field which Abraham purchased from the sons of Heth. There Abraham was buried, and Sarah his wife. And it came to pass, after the death of Abraham, that God blessed his son Isaac. And Isaac dwelt at Beer Lahai Roi" (Gen 25:8-11 NKJV).

Allowing for differences in time and custom, Abraham and Sarah give us a fine example of how to live trusting in God's promise. Saying goodbye isn't easy at any time of life. And the last farewells are no doubt the hardest. But I think God will give us a special grace at the last. I like Tolkien's translation of Gawain's farewell song in *Sir Gawain and the Green Knight*:

> For everything must have an end
> And even friends must part, I fear;

But we beloved however dear
Out of this world death will us reave,
And when we brought are to our bier
Against our will we take our leave.

Though the Mountains May Fall

Going to church with our elder daughter Lucy and our two
grandchildren, Ardis and Avery, is a lovely experience. Recently we smiled when the closing hymn was announced.
"They need guitars," Lucy said. And she was right.

Though the mountains may fall, and the hills turn to dust
Yet the love of the Lord will stand.

We sang it. And we believed it. Nothing could separate us
from the love of God.

Though Scripture and hymns offer us many images of the
life to come, I prefer to focus on God's powerful and everlasting love. It is scattered throughout the Bible: in the
Psalms, in the Prophets, in the promises Jesus gives to us.
God's love is what we cling to in the later years, our hope of
the life to come. As we read in Scripture, "The LORD appeared to us in the past, saying: 'I have loved you with an
everlasting love; I have drawn you with unfailing kindness'"
(Jer 31:3 NIV).

Words to live by. We rise in the dark, anticipating the
dawn. Again, always and again in our later years as in times
past, we are in search of Sunday. Not just this day, but the
Lord's own day. A day of reconciliation and peace.

My soul turns cartwheels. It is not only Sunday, but
Sunday, September 11, 2011. I've been visiting my daughter
Lucy and her kids in Shreveport, where I had the fun of being

with them for an easygoing routine of back to school, evening supper, baths, planning for the morning, homework, visiting and family time. At the supper table, on placemats that say "I love Paris," the four of us talk about the meaning of the week, of the day, of remembrance itself. A snatch of an old song comes back to me. Why, I have no idea.

Show me that river,
Take me across
And wash all my troubles away
While that lucky old sun
Got nothing to do
But roll around heaven all day.

It is a Sunday night, and the following day is Patriots Day. In our family it is a Sabbath time, though we do not frame it in religious talk. Instead, Ardis explains to me how he thinks remembrance works. "You see, I was just a baby. I can't remember, really. But my mother had a hard time. She said it really shook her up. Everything had been quiet and peaceful. It was a blue sky. And then this airplane . . ."

He pauses. Lucy takes up the story. "We were in Alexandria. I had heard it on the radio. The whole office was in shock. Ardis was at home, in his crib, his father was with him, but we felt that everything had gone . . . crazy. All the simplicity and safety we thought we had . . ."

I remembered their sweet little house in Alexandria. Tree-lined street, pretty fences, yard signs for "best house," stones defining the front walk, green shoots coming up between. It was vividly etched in memory. Yes, and the event itself, remembered as Ardis could not—those children who could be shielded, even the infants, were shielded. Yet some say even infants can remember terror—fire blazing, white-hot heat. Couples jumping from upper stories, descending hand in hand.

Helpless, Bill and I watched towers flame, burn, collapse. Our world seemed to be collapsing too. It was strange, dislocating. Where, we wondered, was the strength of our faith to be found, where was there any rock to stand on?

"Let's go to Mass," Lucy had said that day. Oddly, we were afraid to go outside, and the regular hum of the aircraft, hospital helicopters and planes that go overhead, was absent. Everything was grounded. The president was in the air, or was he? No one knew. Our trust was in God. He was our leg to stand on. He was our rock, our stone of comfort, our salvation.

Fifteen minutes later, Lucy was in our doorway. We stood together watching on television a world in flames. "We'll miss the Mass; we have to focus," one of us said. Bill got his coat. I got my cane. Did we take two cars, or one?

All over Alexandria people were gathering to pray. The cathedral bells rang, calling us. Slowly the community assembled. Everyone from both sides of the river, believers and nonbelievers, black and white, mixed, flowing together, everyone from any belief or persuasion, wanting. The longing was powerful. We went like woodpeckers, like mosquito hawks, dragonflies, like bees, homing to the place that was God for us.

People were weeping. A few moaned. We hardly knew what to do or say, but we felt the ritual would sustain us.

The day's readings.
The psalm,
The letters of Paul,

The gospel with its words of forgiveness and
    reconciliation.
Breaking and eating the body of the Lord.
And for those who could not partake,
Even so,
We were made one body by our longing and his Word.
For what his Word doth make it,
That I believe and take it.

Could we convey all this to Ardis, now ten, and Avery, his eight-year-old sister, born since then? We knew we could not. And always the cautionary thought: how much should we convey?

"I wasn't born yet," Avery said brightly, shaking her long, reddish-gold princess hair. She liked her hair and its ornamental way of falling over her shoulders. As we talk she examines the ends of her burnished locks, worried that they are too frizzy, upset that her hair is naturally curly and she wants it to be smooth and straight. But she continues to fill me in on the proper historical self-understanding.

"I wasn't born yet, but Mommy wants to tell me the story, so I will know how she felt on that day. Besides, it's history," she explains to me importantly, and nods to the social studies lesson we had been doing moments before.

"That's one way to do history," Ardis explains further. He is going to be eleven soon. He likes the feeling of knowing, of being in charge. Ardis smooths out his red shirt; he is still in the clothes he wore to football practice. He is munching on broccoli cuts and spaghetti with red meat sauce, resisting the idea of early bed but torn, because he doesn't want to be slow off the mark the next morning.

"Sure you don't want to take your bath tonight?" Lucy says. Suddenly she is not the mourner, the day of remembrance person, but a mother who wants to be sure everyone shows up bright as a button on Patriots Day.

"What do you do on Patriots Day?" I asked the kids, relishing every chance to understand their lives and be in step with them.

"Well, see, everyone wears a certain shirt, and everything sort of matches. It's, you know, patriotic colors, red and blue shirts and all that—"

"But you can't wear your uniform shirt," Avery pipes in, "even if it's white because it has to be a plain white, pure white shirt."

By this time I am really moved. The torn flags of Gettysburg and Shiloh are forming in my mind. And then a sudden biblical leap. Scripture too is embedded in memory: Put on the whole armor of God that you may understand how to resist the snares of the devil. And then a further leap to the prayers and gospels we once said at Sunday Mass: "Holy Michael archangel, defend us in battle. Be our protection against the wickedness and snares of the devil. Do you rebuke him, we humbly pray, and by the pow'r of God cast into hell Satan and all the other devils that roam the world, seeking the ruin of souls."

Had they read that in the cathedral on 9/11? I think they had. Or was it just because in the jumble of the assembly—mourners, bikers, priests and clergy—my mind carried me back to other historic churches and other places where the old prayers were read. Really, I wasn't sure. Memory is a knave and a trickster, jumping back and forth from decade to decade. Fear heightens this "jumping-back, jumping-jack" consciousness. In the suddenly gathered community I imagined other times other moments when fear brought whole communities into focus. Then prayer, unbidden, rose in my heart.

And the Lord whom I so desired was mine already . . .

Lord God, you are my anchor,
My deliverer in times of stress,

I was climbing again the ropes of uncertainty, looking
     for a firm place to stand
And he was mine already,
As in times past
More than beauty
More than music
More than song.

My rock
My Christ
My deliverer
My healer
God in whose palm I rest secure
forever.

Lucy stands up from the table. It's way past our intended bedtime of nine o'clock. It's September, I say to Ardis. It gets late sooner. At once I realize my error but let it stand. It gets dark sooner, it gets late about the same time every day, and late is such a shifting term.

Late have I loved thee
Late of Kings college

I muse over the various meanings of "late" and "lateness." I am conscious that time is precious, slipping through our hands. The children, Lucy and I, all of us are living with the mystery of time. My mind will not let go of it, tracking the language, tracking the memory, tracking the Lord of earth and heaven.

O beauty so ancient, so new
Lord Christ, in light and darkness be present to us.

Ardis turns reluctantly to bath time, wanting to go out in
the yard instead and let the warm darkness fall on him, lose
himself in the dark poultice of the night sky, but he does not.
He turns on his heel and went. I am glad to see the young
man appearing, yet I long to hold on to the dreaming child I
have loved. I pray once again, as in former times, for the Lord
to bring me through the wilderness.

Down by the Riverside

Although Father Val has told us he is facing death, three
years have passed since we first began working with him on
his memoir, his legacy, this project and that. It's hard to
know, especially from his cheerful voice on the phone, when
to worry and when to relax.

But there are warning signs. Clouds darkening. Trouble
brewing. Nancy, his secretary, lets us know that he is failing
through simple observations. She notices what he doesn't
attend—events he never would have missed in earlier years.
She herself is not entirely sure how he is doing, when he will
rally, when the end will come. Bill and I tell ourselves we
should head to New Orleans the first chance we get.

Nancy, who till now has been a voice on the phone, turns
out to be a beauty in a plum-colored dress. Meeting her at a
New Orleans coffeehouse, we decide that a balanced diet of
business, visiting and prayer will be just right. The drive from
Alexandria to New Orleans has been clear sailing, blue skies
and open traffic all the way. But the errand of mercy is real.

Father Val is being treated at Our Lady of Wisdom on the
West Bank. It's a beautiful facility, but Father Val is not just

there for a lark. Because he's so resilient it is sometimes hard to figure out when he is really sick. But Nancy suspects his morale is drooping. Closer to the situation than we are, Nancy assures us that our arrival may have a good effect.

After the visit to Father Val we will head back into downtown New Orleans. We are relieved to find him so well, so able to get up and host us at lunch, so quick to give cheerful commands. "Emilie, maybe you'd like to sit over there. Bill, you'll be at my left here. Shall we ask for some butter, or anything else?"

Father Val asks a blessing and our light conversation begins. The meal is excellent and beautifully served. My gratitude starts to surge. I am grateful to have such a friend as this. To be among his wide circle of admirers, colleagues and conversation partners.

I am glad that we were able to come to lift his spirits. Glad, too, that we have covered our brief agenda, good for morale, his and ours, a way of stretching into the future. Happy to have a keen sense of doing something for God. Something simple. Something just right for us, for who we are. I feel I am basking in a sun patch of consolation, the warmth of the Lord saying, "Yes, Emilie. That's good. Keep on. That's the good way."

The health care facility at Algiers Point is a historic property, restored to reflect the history of New Orleans, the rivers that flow together into the muddy Mississippi. It is a long history stretching back not only to the founding of the city but through the living memories of citizens to Europe and Africa and Asia, Latin America and beyond. Banana plants wave in the sunshine. Green palmettos spread out a sort of leafy fan of energy and joy. Blue skies seem to promise a kind of forever: God's faithfulness even to those in rocking chairs, on walkers or, like me, on a stout cane. Inwardly, the music starts:

> I see trees of green, red roses too,
> A world that will shine for me and for you,
> And I say to myself,
> What a wonderful world . . .

I find myself humming before I even know what the words are. Another song drifts into mind: "As I go down to the river to pray, studying about that good old way . . ."

Bill and I say our goodbyes, stuffing things into our bags— pencils and papers and memos. Bill walks ahead of me through the long, cool corridors and suddenly we come into the light.

The return journey over the Mississippi River Bridge is pleasant, simple, consoling. Skies open up for us into a full canvas of beauty, a landscape and a skyscape of the soul. Going through the tollbooth, reaching for my crumpled dollar, I have a sharp feeling of homewardness, being just where I should be.

It's a grace, I think. I'm walking in grace. Well, driving in it.

The rest of the day yawns ahead, promising naps, more visiting, time with our son Henry and his wife Larisa. "Hang time," as Henry often puts it.

> Oh sister let's go down,
> Down to the river to pray.

The ride over the Crescent City Bridge has a roller coaster feel.

> Sometimes I'm up.
> Sometimes I'm down.

Oh yes Lord
Sometimes I'm almost to the ground
Oh yes Lord.

Gonna lay down my sword and shield
Down by the riverside
Down by the riverside,
Down by the riverside . . .

And I ain' gonna study war no more
I ain' gonna study war no more
I ain' gonna study war no more,
Yes, Lord.

It's a foot-tapper. But the holiness is real. "Gonna lay down my burdens, down by the riverside, down by the riverside."

Look up. Look down. Look all around.
For your salvation is close at hand.
Always, there is the presence and the sunshine of our
    Lord Jesus Christ.
And his simple promise of always,
I am with you always
Yesterday today and forever.
Even unto the end of the world.
Alleluia, alleluia, Amen.

Into the Future

One of the things I love about my life now is the simplicity of it. I love the turn of the earth and the dawn breaking. I love washing apples in the sink, seeing them bob in the water, green and red and gold. Dawn is breaking over the edge of the world and I am part of it, fully present, fully alive. I love the warm smell of biscuits browning and the elegant transparency of grapefruit juice or fizzy water in the glass, the tartness of lime twisted and lying lovely and graceful on the breakfast tray. The shine of a well-washed kitchen table, and the clear coldness of the water pouring over my grateful hands.

I come at last to the knowledge that what we have, all we have, is the present moment, the now. And more than that, the knowledge of God's love and grace opening us up to his unlimited future.

That is the path of wisdom, and I am grateful for it.

But there are deadlines to be met this morning. Things to do. I am dwelling in the present moment and reaching into the future all at once. The day looms, and at some unspecified moment the ring of truth, the noise of practical wisdom—a doorbell, a telephone—will shatter the peaceful silence of my morning.

Joy. Peace. Gratitude. All these, and even in the dark times Christ befriends us. I pray to know this, and to keep on knowing it, as we move into the future.

Reflections, Questions and a Prayer

Are there certain things—traveling, sewing, learning to play an instrument—that you always meant to do in later years? Make a list of them. Are some more practical than others? Consider, within your constraints of time, whether you will explore a new interest or hobby.

Are there some ways you can "cut loose" in the later years? Change your style of dress or make some changes in your appearance? Is this consistent with your ideas of what a Christian should do and be? Discuss, or reflect on this in your journal.

The psychologist Erik Erikson made a study of the later years. He lived into his eighties and suggested that many old people try to resist the appearance of aging—for example, by using a cane instead of a walker—and may impede their own treatment and well-being. What do you think about this idea? Does it apply to you in any way?

What about youthfulness? Is it a matter of outside appearances or inner attitudes? What do you think are the most youthful things about yourself? Can you think of old people you know who seem youthful to you? Why?

What is the value of risk-taking? Is it a physical challenge, or a spiritual one?

How do you experience joy in the later years?

Prayer
Lord, give me curiosity and a sense of adventure. Let me continue to take a chance on love.

APPENDIX

Writing Your Spiritual Autobiography

One way to get a sense of the meaning of long life is to write a memoir. This does not have to be as long as a book, though it may be. Even if you write an essay-length account of your own life, you will begin to get an overview of what it has been "about." Consider writing such a memoir. You may want to dictate your memoir into a tape recorder and then transcribe some of it into written form. Such extended reflection helps you to grasp the meaning of long life, including your long life.

Ask yourself questions like these: What have I done with my life? How many hearts have I mended? How much laughter have I spread? How much tenderness? How much insight? We value these things, and we want to know the grace of what we do and where we go. It is hard to capture one life in words, and we have little objectivity about our own. Yet it matters to see the arc of our life, to be grateful for the richness of God's blessings. Also, take note of the many defeats and failures, not all of which you may have the courage to name. These, too, may be blessings, and the goal is to understand and accept them. Then move on. Look forward, grateful for the blessings of each day and the days to come.

Here is the memoir I wrote. So often I have—in retreats and conferences—advised others to write a full-life memoir. Suddenly, as part of my own self-reflection, I realized I had never actually done this myself. The advice I have given to others is to write first, uncritically letting the events flow. Telling the story. Afterward will come a time for reflection, to read over each section and learn.

Childhood

I had a really privileged childhood—not in terms of material privilege but because of a real spiritual depth. I was born in New Orleans and lived in modest circumstances there. My great-aunt Eula, a schoolteacher, taught me to read at three, and reading became one of my chief pleasures. Sometimes as an only child I felt lonely for companions my own age. Despite having playmates, I didn't find real friendship until about fifth grade, age ten or so, among a circle of girls at Newman School. One of them, Louise Alcus Simon, is still a friend of mine. We take part in a Bible study group of nine members. It's "our" group, in that we founded it and lead it together. But it's also symbolic to me of the lifelong treasure of friendship.

Closeness with my mother was one of my blessings. Her high creativity was a joy. When I was four, she led me on a Halloween jaunt through the uptown sidewalks of New Orleans. I pulled behind me a train of shoeboxes on makeshift wheels. Halloween figures were cut out of the sides of the shoeboxes, and colored cellophane created small illuminated "windows." Together we rescued baby birds that had fallen from the nest and fed them with an eyedropper. Some years later, my mother staged a treasure hunt party with clues leading children around our neighborhood. Friends of mine remembered this event for years.

In sixth or seventh grade I made friends with Paul Marechal, the son of the vice consul of Belgium, who lived across the street. Paul had a sister and a brother, but they were too old to play games with him. Soon he and I entered a world of literary imagination, playing pirate games in which the English Henry Morgan was both protagonist and villain, sacking various cities in the Caribbean. We also did more or less well with the Wild West. At one point Paul and I staged a formal debate (held at our house one evening) about the Spanish Armada. I took the British side and Paul took the side of Spain. I don't remember who won. But Paul certainly should have won because he embodied everything that was romantic and glamorous about the Spanish character. I can still remember how he described the British marauders attacking a Caribbean city called Nombre de Dios ("Name of God," but it sounds so lovely in Spanish!). How in the world does the memory retain such things?

I lost track of Paul when his father was transferred to Washington, D.C., but renewed the friendship many years later in New Orleans when I discovered that Paul was a writer and a man of deep prayer. He is now Brother Elias at a Cistercian abbey in Conyers, Georgia, called Monastery of the Holy Spirit, and he is the author of a beautiful book about the spiritual life titled *Dancing Madly Backwards: A Journey into God*.

Archery and horseback riding were my favorite sports, and I feel sure that their appeal was also part of my literary streak. Shades of Robin Hood and Maid Marian.

My father, Norman Dietrich, was a romantic figure to me, though somewhat distant. I was saddened but not totally surprised when he and my mother were divorced. I was eleven when those proceedings began.

My grandmother Lucy Russell, whom I called "Nui," was a close spiritual friend throughout my childhood. My mother went out to work, and my grandmother stayed at home and cared for me. From my grandmother I learned to love theater, especially musical theater, and poetry. I can still hear her singing the "Vilja song" from *The Merry Widow*: "Vilja, o Vilja, my witch of the wood, would I not die for you, dear, if I could?" When I realized in school that I was good at reciting poetry, I did not recognize at first that my grandmother had helped form me that way. But she had. She also helped to form my love of the Bible and strong Christian faith.

Teen Years

I was thirteen when I entered the Louise S. McGehee school in New Orleans as a freshman. It is a college preparatory school for girls, founded in 1912 by Louise S. McGehee, and in my high school days many New Orleanians still referred to it as "Miss McGehee's." Certainly the strong stamp of her personality was on the school, and her sister Ethel and her niece Elise were both important figures there during my time.

In high school I learned how much I loved languages, so I studied four years of Latin and two years of Spanish. (Meanwhile, I was learning spoken Spanish through my friendship with another diplomatic family, Panamanians named Jimenez who lived across the street from us. They remained lifelong friends.) McGehee's set the bar very high and my teachers demanded a lot. I loved measuring up to their near-impossible demands. In Latin I read Caesar's *Gallic Wars*, some orations of Cicero, and many passages of Virgil. In English class we did Dickens's *Tale of Two Cities* and *Great Expectations*, four plays by Shakespeare, and other plays from across the centuries: from Aeschylus to George Bernard Shaw. In high school I also took acting lessons from my grandmother's friend Maud Drewry, an old woman by then who had performed in repertory in Britain. We used Shakespeare texts for practice, and she taught me how to make an entrance. If I had become an actress, no doubt I would have learned something different later on.

McGehee's was a poor school then, in the sense of equipment, but it was rich in tradition and values. The nativity play at Christmastime was one of the most formative events of my life. I still recall the high voices of the fourth-graders singing "The Friendly Beasts": "I, said the cow, all white and red, I gave him a pillow for his head." Another haunting carol was "Bring a Torch, Jeanette, Isabella" and though our assembly room was the loft of a former carriage house, the illusion was complete: it was on earth, and it was heaven.

I graduated second in my class at McGehee's and gave the valedictory address. Among my prizes were two important books: *The Bible Designed to Be Read as Living Literature* and a book of mystical poems, including one by Henry Vaughan (1622–1695):

I saw eternity the other night
    Like a great ring of pure and endless light,

All calm as it was bright,
And round beneath it time in hours, days, years,
   Driv'n by the spheres,
Like a vast shadow moved in which the world
   And all her train were hurled.

Also, I received a four-year honor scholarship to Newcomb College of Tulane University, entering as a freshman at seventeen. The high literary curve continued in my college days as I read Shakespeare, Milton, Chaucer, John Donne and George Herbert, as well as Wordsworth, Coleridge, and a century's worth of novelists. Because of the way our comprehensive exams were scheduled, I missed James Joyce and Virginia Woolf. So I had to connect with them later on.

Probably my best friend in high school and college was my cousin Dave, whose full name was Henry Davis Prescott Jr. He was my "fourth cousin," I liked to say. Actually my great-grandmother, Sallie Ball Powell, and his grandmother, Eula Ball Prescott, had been sisters. I was struck by him when we first met, at about thirteen or fourteen years of age. He was summoned downstairs by his parents to play the piano for my mother, my grandmother and me. He played Chopin, and very well. He had a biting wit and a love of literature, music and the arts. Soon after that we began going to art films on Sunday nights. We went to college at about the same time and have remained friends over a lifetime.

Mademoiselle Guest Editor: A Turning Point

Though I had traveled before—a cruise from New Orleans to Panama in 1952, a railway trip to Canada in 1953—the most life-changing trip I ever made was to New York City in 1956. I was nineteen, almost twenty, just finishing my junior year at Newcomb, and I had won a contest to become a *Mademoi-selle* magazine guest editor. That high-powered internship, lasting for the month of June, plunged me into a very large world. It was the same ground traveled by Joan Didion, Gloria Steinem, Sylvia Plath.

At the theater I saw Julie Harris in Jean Anouilh's *The Lark*, Jason Robards in *The Ice Man Cometh*, Ruth Gordon, Bobby Morse and Anthony Perkins in *The Matchmaker* (later adapted as *Hello, Dolly*). *Mademoiselle* had arranged for us to have a backstage visit with Ruth Gordon, but first they had to explain to us how important Ruth Gordon was. I interviewed Kermit Bloomgarden, the theater producer who had four shows running at the time. We made a visit to the *New York Times* and met Harvey Breit, editor of the Book Review, and Clifton Daniel, editor of the newspaper. Daniel had just married Margaret Truman that April and the pair had appeared on the cover of *Time* magazine. For the first time I was faced with true celebrity.

Another haunting legend of a person was Madame Helena Rubinstein, who hosted a reception for us in her three-story penthouse on Park Avenue. I was stunned by her—she was dressed *a la chinoise* and held court from an elegant antique sofa at one end of a long mirrored hall. I was also struck by the place itself. There were paintings by Picasso and Dali—painted as murals, directly on the walls. And some of them were signed "To my darling Helena, with love, Pablo." What would it be like, I wondered, to know such people? To be the guardian of such remarkable works of art? At the same time I was conscious that Rubinstein's empire was founded on cold cream. What was I to make of this? Also I was reflecting on Milton's wariness about fame:

Fame is the spur which the clear spirit doth raise
That last infirmity of noble mind
To scorn delights, and live laborious days.

Well, you may say that youth is wasted on the young, but certainly I was attentive to Milton's admonition. He was afraid of his own desire for fame. In his poems he confessed it in a very public way.

One important thing I did in New York City that summer was to visit the Frick collection, Mr. Frick's personal assemblage of great paintings. I saw the portrait of Descartes and one of John Donne. These people had actually lived. Even in their frilly collars, they were astonishingly real. What is greatness? I wondered.

In college I majored in English literature. Even in the theater I found Englishness appealing, doing a minor role in Noel Coward's *Blithe Spirit* and a major role, Mrs. Hardcastle, in Oliver Goldsmith's comedy *She Stoops to Conquer*. I also did four years of Latin, reading Virgil, Cicero, Horace, Ovid, Pliny the Younger, Juvenal, Propertius, Catullus, Livy, Seneca, Plautus and Terence, Lucretius (*On the Nature of Things*) and even Petronius. Fortunately a number of films were made in the 1950s about the ancient world, and I especially recall Leo Genn's amazing portrayal of Petronius, who was called the Arbiter Elegantiarum and served under the emperor Nero.

I also studied Spanish literature, and in my graduation summer (1957) finished that off with studies at the National University of Mexico where I read poetry from the Spanish Golden Age, including Lope de Vega, Garcilaso de la Vega, and Sor Juana Inez de la Cruz. I also studied Federico Garcia

Lorca, a twentieth-century poet and dramatist who was executed during the Spanish Civil War. Those lectures were given in Spanish by a distinguished professor from Madrid. Living with a family in Mexico City helped me to develop real fluency in Spanish. I also survived a full-scale earthquake, saw my first and only bullfight, and caught a sailfish in the waters off Acapulco. After a lovely summer, I knew that I really wanted to live in the U.S.A. after all.

Defeats

Some defeats were in store, despite the honors I had gained at Tulane, despite Phi Beta Kappa. The highest academic honor was a special mention on my comprehensives. The university gave me high recommendations. But I did not win a Marshall Scholarship. I had been dreaming of Cambridge, but did not win a Fulbright. Though I had a scholarship to Tulane's graduate school, I folded my tents. I decided that the life of the mind was not for me. It was years before I understood that I really was a scholar after all.

In the fall of 1957 I joined the *New Orleans Item*, an afternoon daily newspaper, as a reporter. I worked there for half a year and then moved on to a local advertising agency, determined to learn about broadcast media, including television. In my heart I took Milton's words with me: "I cannot praise a fugitive and cloistered virtue."

Twenties

The most decisive decade for me was my twenties. I moved to New York City in 1959 and began to look for a job. My dream was to become a playwright, but I needed an income. Though the wait seemed endless, it was just six weeks till I got a job at Fuller and Smith and Ross advertising, working on corporate and industrial TV advertising. (One observation: after my six-week wait I went into St. Peter's Lutheran Church on Lexington Avenue and prayed for a job. I received an offer in twenty-four hours.) Soon I was going to studios, sitting in on music and voice-over recording sessions, going to shoots on location, sitting in on editing sessions. Within three years I could claim seven Clio awards for an Alcoa Aluminum corporate campaign and one award at the Venice Film Festival. It was heady stuff.

Romance was something of a problem. Though I dated constantly, no one seemed right. One important person was "Ken" Toole, who was more of a friend and dancing partner than a serious love interest. This was John Kennedy Toole, who later wrote the posthumously published and Pulitzer Prize–winning novel *Confederacy of Dunces*. I was engaged to another man briefly, but it didn't work out. I felt lonely and seriously disillusioned, and I felt that my only refuge was in God.

But was God real or just a comfortable illusion? I was confused about that and went on a pilgrimage of sorts through reading. Eventually I sought instruction and received excellent teaching from a young Anglican priest, Father Charles Owen Moore, at the Church of the Resurrection in Manhattan. I was eventually baptized there, in 1962. My religious journey continued and swept me into the Roman Catholic Church, which received me in 1963.

A number of authors influenced me with their published sermons or conversion stories. C. S. Lewis was important. I read *Mere Christianity*, *Surprised by Joy*, *The Screwtape Letters*, *The Four Loves*, *Miracles* and *The Problem of Pain*. All of it helped me to decide that thinking modern people could be Christian believers. Thomas Merton and others were also influential. Ronald Knox and G. K. Chesterton attracted me to Roman Catholic faith.

I pursued the playwright's journey as well. In November 1961 I joined a class taught by Edward Albee at the Circle in the Square in Greenwich Village. I wrote my first play, a one-act, called *The Remarkable Thanksgiving of Charity Ward*, heavily influenced by Thornton Wilder and Albee himself. The theater of the absurd was in full swing, and I wondered whether I should follow its lead.

In the Albee class I met a young writer named (as I then thought) Hilary Griffin. His real name was Henry William Griffin, and most of his life he has been called either "William" or "Bill." We fell in love. We were married in August 1963, and the marriage has had staying power. Bill's one-act for the Albee class was called *The Omega Point* and was inspired by the thought of Pierre Teilhard de Chardin, of whom I had never heard. The writing was brilliant. It seemed we were both on our way.

After our marriage, we both wrote full-length plays in a tiny apartment in Brooklyn. Mine, called *The Only Begotten Son*, was about a tragic New Orleans family, a father-and-son conflict. It won the first playscript award from the Louisiana Council of Performing Arts in 1971 but was never produced. The racial tensions reflected in the play were too mild for Broadway and too intense for New Orleans.

Bill's first play, *A Fourth for the Eighth*, came closer to success. It was optioned for Broadway almost at once. But soon it hit a snag. Bill's play was about Henry VIII and Anne of Cleves. That same year, a play by Anita Loos on the same subject had been produced in London. So Bill's play lost ground. Our agent at the time was Ann Elmo, who believed in us. "Never give up," she said with a kind of Churchillian zeal.

Meanwhile we both continued working in our day jobs, mine in advertising and Bill's in publishing. He worked at Macmillan, at Harcourt, then at Macmillan again. I left Fuller and Smith and Ross in 1964 and continued in advertising at Compton.

Thirties

In July 1966 I turned thirty. That year Bill and I went to England for the first time and spent three amazing weeks seeing the places we cared about. He was writing a play about the Jesuit Edmund Campion, who was martyred under Queen Elizabeth I, so we went to the Tower of London, where Campion had been imprisoned. It was a glorious round of visits to Westminster Abbey, Westminster Cathedral, Hampton Court, places both Protestant and Catholic, an array of visits to theaters new and old, to Chichester, Hastings, Bath, Stratford on Avon, Oxford, Cambridge and back to London again.

I made a visit to the London office of my advertising agency, Compton, and sat in on a creative session. We went to Carnaby Street, which was all the rage, and I went for a haircut to Vidal Sassoon. The sixties were changing every-thing. But one thing became clear to us. We had waited long enough for a family. In the years 1968, 1969 and 1971 our three children were born. By then we were living in tight quarters in a small apartment in Queens, but having our new family was the answer to a prayer.

My business life changed radically. In 1969 (after five years) I was named a vice president of Compton Advertising. In 1970, with two young children in hand, I was fired and went to work as a consultant at General Foods in White Plains while waiting for my third child to be born.

After Sarah arrived we had an eventful summer. Bill's play, *Campion*, was chosen to be staged by the Eugene O'Neill festival, and Sarah (about six weeks old) and I went along. Again it seemed we would become Broadway or at least Off Broadway playwrights.

In October 1971 I was hospitalized for problems related to stress. During my recovery I decided that for the next few years I would stay home with my young children. Work and career were fine, but nothing was more important to me than that little crew.

By the time Sarah, our youngest, was three, we were able to buy a large and comfortable house in Kew Gardens, Queens. I went back to work, not in advertising but in a policy-related job at the Council of Better Business Bureaus; my work centered on children and television.

I was introduced to our industry supporters in a meeting at the Harvard Club. I went to Washington a lot, spoke at conferences and to parent groups, and was interviewed on radio and television and by the *New York Times*. I put together a distinguished committee of advisors, including Dr. Gerry Lesser of Harvard, one of the architects of *Sesame Street*. Thinking about the future of children and media was demanding. Ultimately the work on policy issues (writing testimony, giving speeches) gave me the confidence to go back to my own writing.

In the early 1970s I began to write fiction. In the later

1970s I wrote a book about conversion that was published by Doubleday and praised in the *New York Times*. Meanwhile, Bill was gaining visibility as an editor. He worked with many distinguished authors, from Mortimer Adler to Elizabeth Kubler Ross, but his work with the C. S. Lewis backlist put him front and center, and his work was much admired in the press. He was also a second-night theater critic and a member of the Drama Critics' Circle, which bestows the Tony awards.

It was hard raising three young children in New York City, with two jobs and a live-in helper (and her child, making four children in all), but it had certain rewards. I ended the decade by going back to work at Compton Advertising, being named a VP again, having flowers on my desk and being told "This time it's going to be different." It wasn't. They fired me a second time in 1980, and I was "on the road again." *Turning*, my book on conversion, was published later that year. I thought it would move me in new directions, and it did.

Forties

I'm not sure exactly when I discovered "the spiritual life." Probably 1975 or 1976. But it was deeply strengthening. I began to go to weekday Mass and I often went into churches at lunchtime to pray. I began to make retreats. It was a deepening of the Christian life I already had. Also I began to read the devotional classics, Francis de Sales, Jean-Pierre de Caussade, Evelyn Underhill and a Belgian Cistercian named Andre Louf. These were slender books but very inviting. They slipped easily into my briefcase. I read *The Cloud of Unknowing* and thought it was beautiful. I began to seek spiritual direction from a Catholic priest I knew. He is the one who, in a sermon preached before I even knew his name, had encouraged me in the spiritual life.

New York City offered opportunities to hear talks by and about major theologians. At Union Theological Seminary, I attended a daylong seminar on Dietrich Bonhoeffer led by the eminent Bonhoeffer scholar Eberhard Bethge. On another occasion I played hooky from the office for a day in order to hear a four-hour talk by Hans Kung.

During the mid-1970s Bill and I became active members of the New York C. S. Lewis Society. We gave presentations and our talks were published in the society's bulletin. My love of C. S. Lewis, which had begun in the 1960s, was confirmed. It was a blessing to know others who cared about Lewis and hear about which books had influenced them.

In 1980 we decided to move to New Orleans, partly because my mother needed us and partly because we needed a fresh start. Macmillan was loath to let go of Bill. It took a while to sell our house in New York City. We bought a house in New Orleans and put the children in school there before the New York house was sold. All in all it took us almost a year to make the change.

Macmillan gave Bill a contract to write a new biography of C. S. Lewis. *Publishers Weekly* put him under contract as editor of religious books, an arrangement that lasted twelve years. Bill began spending part of his time in Britain, interviewing people who had known Lewis and getting more familiar with many Lewis texts.

I wrote a slender book on prayer, called *Clinging*, that was published by Harper in San Francisco. Bill wrote his Lewis biography, which was eventually published as *Clive Staples Lewis: A Dramatic Life*. The British edition was called *C. S. Lewis: The Authentic Voice*.

During the 1980s, while working full time, Bill and I both did theology studies at the Catholic seminary in New Orleans and at Loyola. As part of that, I did a two-year independent study in philosophy, reading Plato, Aristotle, Augustine, Thomas Aquinas, Bonaventure and others, ten in all including Bernard Lonergan and Alfred North Whitehead. These philosophy studies strengthened me. Another modern Catholic theologian who strongly impressed me was Karl Rahner. In a semester on "Theology of Grace" we read Augustine, Aquinas and Luther, and we heard both Roman Catholic and Lutheran professors comment on the growing reconciliation of teaching on justification. In 1986 Bill and I also became founding members of a new group of writers of Christian faith called The Chrysostom Society.

Throughout the 1980s I worked in New Orleans advertising and won a total of fifty creative awards. I wanted to do more of my own writing, but I was strict about giving an honest day's work for my paycheck.

Fifties
Speaking was not my first calling at that time. But somehow speaking helped to focus what I believed in. I remember warmly that I gave the Hugh McCloskey Evans Lecture at Tulane in 1988. The title was "This I Believe: Propositions Regarding the Necessity of Reinventing God." By "reinventing" I meant passionately and creatively reappropriating one's faith. Looking back, it seems like a turning point, a time when doubt gave way to hope. Three eminent Jesuits from Loyola New Orleans were sitting on the front row. They listened to my lecture; they looked at other texts I had written; they encouraged me to continue my work.

In 1990, after publication of my third book, *Chasing the Kingdom*, my employer let me go. Now I was free to set up a freelance practice, hoping that I would one day become a book writer full time. I moved out into a new decade by writing two books, one a spirituality of business and enterprise called *The Reflective Executive*. This book emerged from several major addresses I had given to business leaders as well as two courses taught on "spirituality in the marketplace" at Loyola New Orleans. A second book, on spirituality and aging, was published just six months later. But 1993 and 1994 were hard years for us because of my mother's failing health. My elder daughter's marriage, in June 1994, was followed just two weeks later by my mother's death.

Throughout the nineties I continued to work and write. In 1994 I became active with Richard Foster's group, Renovaré, an international Christian organization currently based in Denver, Colorado.

Sixties and Seventies

With Renovaré, I have written books and appeared at about thirty local, regional, national and international conferences held throughout the United States and in Canada and Britain. I have also written books on prayer, on mysticism, on the observance of such sacred seasons as Christmas, Lent and Easter. I edited and contributed to a book from the Chrysostom Society about writing, including contributions from twenty established writers of faith. The volume you're now reading is the second of two books on spirituality of the later years. I serve on the editorial team for *Conversations: A Forum for Authentic Transformation*, published twice yearly, and as part of the teaching team for the Renovaré Institute.

I have been hospitalized twice for rheumatoid arthritis, once for surgery to repair a fracture, and sometimes for rehabilitation. I have also been active in local groups in the city of Alexandria, Louisiana, where I live. Over and above all these, I have led retreats and served as a spiritual director. My husband and I have been active playwrights in an Alexandria theater group called Spectral Sisters Productions. They have produced a number of his short plays and two ten-minute comedies of mine.

What did I learn in the writing of this memoir? First of all, I noticed the good I had done with my life. Which surprised me. Like many others, I am inclined to think I haven't done enough with my talent and my life. I haven't measured up to the blessings and graces God has given me.

It's true, of course, that I'll never be really good enough to earn the Lord's affections. They're freely given, a grace and a mercy beyond knowing. But sinner that I am, always falling short, I still have done a bit to love others. To befriend them. To live as Jesus did. When I read my own life story, I forgave myself. And I thanked the Lord for all his manifold blessings to me.

Books on the Later Years

Albom, Mitch. *Tuesdays with Morrie*. New York: Doubleday, 1997. A young man captures the last days of his beloved professor in a series of interviews.

Bowles, Peter. *Ask Me If I'm Happy*. London: Simon & Schuster, 2011. This autobiography by a British actor is candid about missed opportunities and the dream of success. Ultimately Bowles chooses God and chooses to be happy.

Carter, Jimmy. *The Virtues of Aging*. New York: Ballantine, 1998. Former President Carter may not be everyone's favorite politician, but in this brief book he shows how he and his wife turned around a bad attitude after their abrupt retirement from the White House.

Chittister, Joan. *The Gift of Years*. New York: BlueBridge, 2008. A much discussed exploration of the gift of long life by a sometimes controversial Benedictine sister.

Cicero. "On Friendship," "On Old Age." In *On Old Age, and On Friendship*. Translated by Frank Olin Copley. Ann Arbor: University of Michigan Press, 1967. Both of these remarkable essays have helped to form Christian ideas about long life and living virtuously and well.

Eliot, T. S. "Gerontion," "The Love Song of J. Alfred Prufrock." In *The Waste Land and Other Poems*. New York: Harcourt, Brace, Jovanovich, 1962. The Nobel Prize–winning poet, playwright and critic reflected some of the angst of living after World War I but wrote poems of great Christian depth about old age.

Erikson, Erik, Joan Erikson and Helen Kivnick. *Vital Involvement in Old*

Age. New York: Norton, 1986. In this book and *The Life Cycle Completed* (see next entry), Erikson shows a strong appreciation of the teachings of Jesus. In these two books on the later years, written with his wife Joan, he reflects on long life, debility and hope.

Erikson, Erik, and Joan Erikson. *The Life Cycle Completed*. New York: Norton, 1997.

Forest, Jim. *The Road to Emmaus*. Maryknoll, N.Y.: Orbis, 2007. Jim Forest, once a colleague of Dorothy Day, has written a fine memoir that deals in part with his own kidney disease and treatment. It is about gratitude and faith.

Foster, Nathan. *Wisdom Chaser*. Downers Grove, Ill.: IVP Books, 2010. In this informal memoir, Nathan Foster recounts a mountain hike in the Rockies with his famous father, Richard Foster, author of many fine books on spiritual life including *A Celebration of Discipline*. It's a worthwhile exploration of how wisdom passes from father to son.

Graham, Billy. *Just As I Am*. San Francisco: HarperSanFrancisco, 1997. The eminent evangelist reflects on a long life with humor and honesty.

Griffin, Emilie. *Souls in Full Sail: Christian Spirituality for the Later Years*. Downers Grove, Ill.: IVP Books, 2010. My own book on getting older. The present volume is a kind of sequel.

James, P. D. *Time to Be in Earnest*. New York: Knopf, 2000. The detective storywriter wrote this account of a year in her life as she approached her eightieth birthday. She has since turned ninety.

Kübler-Ross, Elisabeth. *The Wheel of Life*. New York: Scribner, 1997. A brief memoir on the life cycle by the expert on death and dying.

Leckey, Dolores. *Grieving with Grace*. Cincinnati, Ohio: St. Anthony Messenger Press, 2008. Dolores Leckey, an eminent Catholic laywoman, reflects on the loss of her husband, Tom.

Lewis, C. S. *The Problem of Pain*. San Francisco: HarperSanFrancisco, 2001. *A Grief Observed*. New York: Seabury, 1961. Both these books by C. S. Lewis help us to deal with the more baffling aspects of God.

McInnes, Val A. *Resurrection Fern*. New Orleans: Southern Dominican Books, 2010. A Dominican priest in his eighties tells charming stories about his life and his battle with a rare blood disease. A strong memoir of Christian faith.

Shakespeare, William. *King Lear.* New Haven, Conn.: Yale University Press, 1947. Shakespeare's enduring play offers deep insight into the vulnerability and pitfalls of old age.

Spark, Muriel. *Memento Mori.* Philadelphia: Lippincott, 1959. This brief and comic novel, written when Spark was a young woman, depicts a number of older people coping with the fact of death.

Stannard, Martin. *Muriel Spark: The Biography.* New York: Norton, 2010. Stannard does a good job of tracing the patterns in Spark's long creative life of 88 years and her conversion to Christian Catholic faith.

Whitehead, James and Evelyn. *Christian Life Patterns.* Garden City, N.Y.: Doubleday, 1979. A classic treatment of Christian life stages.

Yancey, Philip. *Where Is God When It Hurts?* Grand Rapids: Zondervan, 1977. Yancey asks the hard questions that Christian believers must ask.

Notes

Preface

Page 12   "Whether it is by learning": Oliver Sacks, "This Year, Change Your Mind," *New York Times,* December 31, 2010 <www.ny times.com/2011/01/01/opinion/01sacks.html?pagewanted=all>.

Chapter 1: Pushing Past the Pain

Page 23   It was a role: Bill Keller, "Morgan Freeman's Long Walk to Nelson Mandela," *Guardian,* December 31, 2009 <www .guardian.co.uk/film/2009/dec/31/morgan-freeman-nelson-mandela-invictus>.

Chapter 2: Blue Skies, Gray Skies

Pages 29-30   "This past year": Bill Vaswig, *Preaching and Prayer Ministries* newsletter, July-August 2010, p. 2.

Page 30   Agnes Sanford: Agnes Sanford, the wife of an Episcopal priest, was a key figure in the charismatic movement in the United States during the 1960s and 1970s. She is probably best known for her book *The Healing Light* (New York: Ballantine, 1983).

Page 33   I think of Ruth Bell Graham: This account of Ruth Bell Graham is drawn from Billy Graham's autobiography, *Just As I Am* (San Francisco: HarperSanFrancisco, 1997) and from Ruth Graham's obituary by Richard Severo, "Wife of Rev. Billy Graham Dies at 87," *New York Times,* June 15, 2007 <www .nytimes.com/2007/06/15/obituaries/15graham.html>.

Page 35   "It was common": Quoted in Severo, "Wife of Rev. Billy Graham Dies."

Page 36   "Then the goodbyes come": Ruth Bell Graham, quoted in ibid.

Page 36   "Ruth is my soul mate": Billy Graham, quoted by Meghan
               Kleppinger, "Ruth Bell Graham: A Legacy of Faith," Christi-
               anity.com, June 18, 2007 <www.christianity.com/Christian
               %20Foundations/The%20Essentials/11544172/>.

Page 40   "Today, James still emanates": P. D. James, quoted by Carol
               Memmott, "P. D. James Solves the Mystery of Living a Full
               Life," *USA Today*, July 20, 2010 <www.usatoday.com/life/
               books/news/2010-07-20-james20_CV_N.htm>.

Chapter 3: Stretching Toward Happiness

Page 46   "I believe I am nearer to God": Jean Renoir, *Renoir, My Father*
               (New York: New York Review Books, 2001).

Page 47   "Never liked to give any sign": Ibid., p. 25.

Page 49   "Beauty remains, but pain passes": Paulo Coelho, "Matisse and
               Renoir Meet," Paulo Coelho's Blog, November 21, 2010.

Page 49   "From the moment he made": Renoir, *Renoir, My Father,* p.
               421.

Page 53   "In this still life": John Nolan, Saatchi Online, October 4,
               2010 <www.saatchionline.com/art/Unknown-Still-Life-With
               -Matisse/296/722251/view>.

Page 53   "A pair of scissors": Ibid.

Page 55   "Spiritual life as pilgrimage": Jim Forest, *The Road to Emmaus*
               (Maryknoll, N.Y.: Orbis, 2007).

Page 55   "If you wish to be sure": John of the Cross, epigraph in
               Forest, *Road to Emmaus,* p. 85.

Page 56   "O God, / It seems like yesterday": William Barclay, "For
               One Who Has Realized He Is Growing Old," in *Prayers for
               Help and Healing* (New York: Harper and Row, 1968), p. 54.

Page 58   Peter Bowles, the British actor: Peter Bowles, *Ask Me If I'm
               Happy* (London: Simon & Schuster, 2011).

Page 58   "Although I'm not a religious man": Peter Bowles, "Confessions
               of Mr Debonair," Mail Online, *Daily Mail,* April 9, 2010 <www
               .dailymail.co.uk/tvshowbiz/article-1264912/Peter-Bowles
               -reveals-misadventures-celebrity-friends-memoirs.html>.

Page 59   "It's a very encouraging fact": Nicholas Bakalar, "Happiness
               May Come with Age, Study Says," *New York Times*, May 31,
               2010 <www.nytimes.com/2010/06/01/health/research/01happy
               .html>.

Chapter 4: Grief, Loss, Anger

Page 66   "Q. How do you feel": Dave Itzkoff, "Woody Allen on Faith, Fortune Tellers and New York," *New York Times*, September 15, 2010 <www.nytimes.com/2010/09/15/movies/15woody.html>.

Page 69   "What balances the movie": Stephen Holden, "Magician's Twisting Road Comes to Bittersweet End," *New York Times*, April 17, 2009 <movies.nytimes.com/2009/04/17/movies/17 ther.html>.

Page 69   "The question I framed": Dolores Leckey, *Grieving with Grace: A Woman's Perspective* (Cincinnati, Ohio: St. Anthony Messenger Press, 2008), p. xvi.

Page 70   "At first it was overwhelming": Ibid., p. xvii.

Page 70   "This is an especially important day": Ibid., p. 30.

Page 71   "Youth is the time for certainties": P. D. James, *Time to Be in Earnest* (New York: Knopf, 2000), p. 240.

Page 71   "There is no point": Ibid., p. 37.

Chapter 5: The Sustaining Grace of Friends

Page 76   "Not long before the day": Augustine, *Confessions,* trans. R. S. Pine-Coffin (New York: Penguin, 1961), pp. 196-97.

Chapter 6: Resetting Goals and Picking Up the Pieces

Page 82   I came across his book: Peter Drucker, *The Effective Executive* (San Francisco: Harper & Row, 1966).

Page 83   In a tribute to Peter Drucker: David Maister, "What Did You Learn from Drucker?" blog entry, April 18, 2007, <www.davidmaister.com/blog/385>.

Page 84   "During these early years": Gayle Beebe, *The Shaping of an Effective Leader: Eight Formative Principles of Leadership* (Downers Grove, Ill.: IVP Books, 2011), p. 14.

Page 89   *BusinessWeek* cover story: John A. Byrne, "The Man Who Invented Management," *BusinessWeek*, November 28, 2005 <www.businessweek.com/magazine/content/05_48/b3961001.htm>.

Page 91   "On November 11, 2005": Beebe, *Shaping of an Effective Leader*, p. 17.

Chapter 7: Age

Page 96   "Age, not youth": Edward Petherbridge, "September Song," Petherbridge's Weekly Post, September 12, 2010 <pether

bridgesweeklypost.blogspot.com/2010/09/september-song
.html>. Used by permission.

Page 96   "And then I see": Ibid.

Page 98   "Tired, I must go to bed": Edward Petherbridge, "Finding a
               Voice," Petherbridge's Weekly Post, August 2, 2010 <pether
               bridgesweeklypost.blogspot.com/2010/08/finding-voice
               .html>.

Page 98   "The thought came to me": Avery Dulles, A Testimonial to
               Grace (New York: Shead & Ward, 1946), pp. 50-51.

Page 101   "One of the greatest thinkers": Joseph Bottum, "Avery Car-
               dinal Dulles," On the Square: Daily Columns from First
               Things' Top Writers, First Things, December 15, 2008 <www
               .firstthings.com/onthesquare/2008/12/avery-cardinal-dulles>.

Page 108   "It was the Sermon on the Mount": Martin Luther King Jr.,
               Stride Toward Freedom: The Montgomery Story, in Spiritual
               Classics, ed. Richard J. Foster and Emilie Griffin (New York:
               HarperOne, 2000), p. 279.

Page 108   "Along the way of life": Ibid., pp. 280-81.

Chapter 8: Following Christ

Page 115   "When one of our friends": Jimmy Carter, The Virtues of
               Aging (New York: Ballantine, 1998), p. 3.

Page 116   "There were other reasons": Ibid., p. 2.

Page 117   "We felt that nothing": Ibid., pp. 3-4.

Page 118   "As we entered our seventies": Ibid., p. 8.

Page 119   Ten most powerful people: Nicole Perlroth and Michael
               Noer, eds., "The World's Most Powerful People," Forbes, No-
               vember 2, 2011 <www.forbes.com/powerful-people/>.

Page 119   In a visit to St. Peter's Residence: Benedict XVI, "Visit to St
               Peter's Residence Care Home and Address to Child Pro-
               tection Personnel, Vauxhall, 18 September 2010," The Tablet,
               September 18, 2010 <www.thetablet.co.uk/page/residence>.

Page 121   "I admire thee": Gerard Manley Hopkins, "The Wreck of the
               Deutschland," in Gerard Manley Hopkins: The Major Works
               (New York: Oxford University Press, 2009), p. 118.

Page 121   "This plant is a symbol": Val A. McInnes, Resurrection Fern
               (New Orleans: Southern Dominican Books, 2010), prolog.

Page 122   "Visible sign of the invisible": Ibid.

Page 122   "Next day we had an appointment": Ibid., p. 133.

Chapter 9: Forever, Just Over There

Page 130   "The last time I read it": Herbert Stein, "On Rereading 'De Senectute,'" *Slate*, November 27, 1998 <www.slate.com/articles/business/it_seems_to_me/1998/11/on_rereading_de_senectute.html>.

Page 133   "When I am an old woman": Jenny Joseph, "Warning: When I Am an Old Woman I Shall Wear Purple," in *Warning: When I Am an Old Woman I Shall Wear Purple* (London: Souvenir, 2001), p. 29.

Page 133   A similar note: T. S. Eliot, "The Love Song of J. Alfred Prufrock."

Page 134   "One step enough": John Henry Newman, "The Pillar of Cloud," in *Hymns of the Christian Church*, The Harvard Classics Vol. 45 Part 2, ed. Charles W. Eliot (New York: Collier and Son, 1909) <www.bartleby.com/45/2/134.html>.

Page 138   He spent his own time: John Henry Newman, *An Essay on the Development of Christian Doctrine* (Cambridge: Cambridge University Press, 2010).

Page 140   "God has appointed me": John Henry Newman, "Meditations on Christian Doctrine," *Newman Reader*, March 7, 1848 <www.newmanreader.org/works/meditations/meditations9.html>.

Page 141   "For everything must have an end": *Sir Gawain and the Green Knight; Pearl; Sir Orfeo*, trans. and ed. J. R. R. Tolkien (New York: Del Rey, 1979), p. 214. A good definition of the archaic word *reave* is "to seize and carry off forcibly."

Page 142   "Though the mountains": Dan Schutte, "Though the Mountains May Fall," OCP Publications, 1975.

Page 143   "Show me that river": Beasley Smith and Haven Gillespie, "That Lucky Old Sun," Emi Robbins Catalog Inc., Haven Gillespie Music, 1949.

Page 150   "As I go down": "Down to the River to Pray," traditional Appalachian song.

Page 150   Bill walks ahead: Father Val McInnes died peacefully on November 22, 2011, at Our Lady of Wisdom on the west bank of New Orleans.

Pages 150-51   "Sometimes I'm up": "Down by the Riverside," traditional gospel song.

Appendix

Page 158   "I saw eternity the other night": Henry Vaughan, "The World," in *The Oxford Book of English Mystical Verse*, ed. D. H. S. Nicholson and A. H. E. Lee (Oxford: Clarendon, 1917) <www.bartleby.com/236/38.html>.

Page 162   "I cannot praise": John Milton, *Prose Writings* (London: Everyman's Library, 1958), p. 158. The quotation is from Milton's address to Parliament known as The Areopagitica.

Page 169   I gave the Hugh McCloskey Evans lecture: Emilie Griffin, "This I Believe: Propositions Regarding the Necessity of Reinventing God," in *Reasoned Faith*, ed. Frank T. Birtel (New York: Crossroad, 1993), pp. 171-82.

Page 170   My elder daughter's marriage: Lucy graduated from Louisiana State University and then earned a degree as a lawyer from Loyola New Orleans. Henry graduated from Loyola University New Orleans with a major in English and has pursued a career in film-making. Sarah's degree is from Newcomb College, Tulane University.

About the Author

Emilie Griffin, a native of New Orleans, lives and writes in Alexandria, Louisiana. She is a member of the Renovaré ministry team and of the Chrysostom Society, a national group for writers of faith. She serves on the editorial team of *Conversations: A Forum for Authentic Transformation*. She has spoken and lectured in various settings and has written a number of books about faith.

formatio

TRADITION. EXPERIENCE.
TRANSFORMATION.

Formatio books from InterVarsity Press follow the rich tradition of the church in the journey of spiritual formation. These books are not merely about being informed, but about being transformed by Christ and conformed to his image. Formatio stands in InterVarsity Press's evangelical publishing tradition by integrating God's Word with spiritual practice and by prompting readers to move from inward change to outward witness. InterVarsity Press uses the chambered nautilus for Formatio, a symbol of spiritual formation because of its continual spiral journey outward as it moves from its center. We believe that each of us is made with a deep desire to be in God's presence. Formatio books help us to fulfill our deepest desires and to become our true selves in light of God's grace.